HAMAS' BENEFACTORS: A NETWORK OF TERROR

JOINT HEARING

BEFORE THE

SUBCOMMITTEE ON
THE MIDDLE EAST AND NORTH AFRICA

AND THE

SUBCOMMITTEE ON TERRORISM,
NONPROLIFERATION, AND TRADE

OF THE

COMMITTEE ON FOREIGN AFFAIRS
HOUSE OF REPRESENTATIVES

ONE HUNDRED THIRTEENTH CONGRESS

SECOND SESSION

_____

SEPTEMBER 9, 2014

_____

Serial No. 113–213

_____

Printed for the use of the Committee on Foreign Affairs

Available via the World Wide Web: http://www.foreignaffairs.house.gov/ or
http://www.gpo.gov/fdsys/

_____

U.S. GOVERNMENT PRINTING OFFICE

89–738PDF   WASHINGTON : 2014

For sale by the Superintendent of Documents, U.S. Government Printing Office
Internet: bookstore.gpo.gov   Phone: toll free (866) 512–1800; DC area (202) 512–1800
Fax: (202) 512–2104   Mail: Stop IDCC, Washington, DC 20402–0001

COMMITTEE ON FOREIGN AFFAIRS

EDWARD R. ROYCE, California, *Chairman*

CHRISTOPHER H. SMITH, New Jersey
ILEANA ROS-LEHTINEN, Florida
DANA ROHRABACHER, California
STEVE CHABOT, Ohio
JOE WILSON, South Carolina
MICHAEL T. McCAUL, Texas
TED POE, Texas
MATT SALMON, Arizona
TOM MARINO, Pennsylvania
JEFF DUNCAN, South Carolina
ADAM KINZINGER, Illinois
MO BROOKS, Alabama
TOM COTTON, Arkansas
PAUL COOK, California
GEORGE HOLDING, North Carolina
RANDY K. WEBER SR., Texas
SCOTT PERRY, Pennsylvania
STEVE STOCKMAN, Texas
RON DeSANTIS, Florida
DOUG COLLINS, Georgia
MARK MEADOWS, North Carolina
TED S. YOHO, Florida
SEAN DUFFY, Wisconsin
CURT CLAWSON, Florida

ELIOT L. ENGEL, New York
ENI F.H. FALEOMAVAEGA, American
  Samoa
BRAD SHERMAN, California
GREGORY W. MEEKS, New York
ALBIO SIRES, New Jersey
GERALD E. CONNOLLY, Virginia
THEODORE E. DEUTCH, Florida
BRIAN HIGGINS, New York
KAREN BASS, California
WILLIAM KEATING, Massachusetts
DAVID CICILLINE, Rhode Island
ALAN GRAYSON, Florida
JUAN VARGAS, California
BRADLEY S. SCHNEIDER, Illinois
JOSEPH P. KENNEDY III, Massachusetts
AMI BERA, California
ALAN S. LOWENTHAL, California
GRACE MENG, New York
LOIS FRANKEL, Florida
TULSI GABBARD, Hawaii
JOAQUIN CASTRO, Texas

AMY PORTER, *Chief of Staff*   THOMAS SHEEHY, *Staff Director*
JASON STEINBAUM, *Democratic Staff Director*

CONTENTS

HAMAS' BENEFACTORS: A NETWORK OF TERROR

TUESDAY, SEPTEMBER 9, 2014

HOUSE OF REPRESENTATIVES,
SUBCOMMITTEE ON THE MIDDLE EAST AND NORTH AFRICA AND
SUBCOMMITTEE ON TERRORISM, NONPROLIFERATION, AND TRADE,
COMMITTEE ON FOREIGN AFFAIRS,
Washington, DC.

The committees met, pursuant to notice, at 10 o'clock a.m., in room 2172 Rayburn House Office Building, Hon. Ileana Ros-Lehtinen (chairman of the subcommittee) presiding.

Ms. ROS-LEHTINEN. The joint subcommittee will come to order.

After recognizing myself, Chairman Poe, Ranking Member Deutch, and Ranking Member Sherman for our opening statements, I will then recognize other members seeking recognition. We will then hear from our distinguished panel of witnesses. And without objection, the witnesses' prepared statements will be made a part of the record, and members may have 5 days in which to insert statements and questions for the record, subject to the length limitation in the rules.

The Chair now recognizes herself for 5 minutes.

ISIL, al-Qaeda, Hezbollah, Hamas—these are some of the most dangerous terrorist groups out today. Though they have all of their differences, notably different ideologies, different objectives, what they do have in common is that they are all non-state actors who need to get their resources from somewhere.

We are now just 2 weeks into the open-ended ceasefire agreement between Israel and Hamas. In the previous 2 months, Hamas terrorists have fired over 4,500 rockets indiscriminately into Israel, including into its most populated areas such as Jerusalem and Tel Aviv.

Of course, it isn't forgotten that the start of these attacks coincided with the abduction and murder of three innocent Israeli teenagers. Hamas originally denied its complicity in this heinous crime but last month admitted responsibility, and it is important to note when this admission took place and by whom.

The announcement was made by a known terrorist and Hamas operative in Turkey where he lives openly. This is the same Turkey that is a supposed U.S. and NATO ally that is harboring not just this member of Hamas, but it is known to be harboring several of Hamas' top operatives.

But harboring these terrorists isn't where Turkey stops. It provides financial, material, and political support for this U.S. designated foreign terrorist organization and has been doing so for years without repercussions. In fact, in 2011, Turkish Prime Minister Erdogan said, ''Hamas is not a terrorist organization. It is a political party.''

But Turkey isn't the only U.S. ally, or at least U.S. partner, that has been known to harbor Hamas leadership and provide the terrorist group with funds. Qatar, the very same Qatar that the administration entrusted to monitor the Taliban five, who were swapped for Sergeant Bergdahl, and which it recently agreed to an $11 billion armed sale with, has been known to be perhaps the largest financial patron of Hamas.

Not only does Qatar harbor Hamas figurehead Khaled Meshaal, Qatar reportedly threatened to exile him if Hamas accepted an Egyptian-backed cease fire agreement last month. In 2011, the Emir of Qatar was the first head of state to visit Gaza and pledged over $400 million of infrastructure money to Hamas. Qatar funds Hamas' strikes in Gaza, as well as its project, building terror tunnels from which to attack Israel rather than building up Gaza for the Palestinian people.

The administration took a step to block a recent transfer of funds from Qatar to Hamas terrorists, and earlier this year the Treasury Department openly admitted that Qatar for many years has openly financed Hamas. It is also supporting extremist groups operating in Syria and has become such a permissive terrorist financing environment for all of these groups, and that includes its funding of the Muslim Brotherhood, and, along with Kuwait, has become a major source of funding for ISIL, a threat that must be eliminated.

According to reports, Egypt has charged former leader Mohamed Morsi with giving national security documents to Qatar, and Qatari connections to the Brotherhood are deep and troubling. But the administration has not done nearly enough to curb Qatari support for terror.

We cannot continue to allow Qatari funds to go to terrorist groups, Hamas or any other, unabated and unaddressed. Yet we have been setting the example for the Qataris and the Turks with how the administration is dealing with Iran. Iran has long been a U.S.-designated state sponsor of terrorism and has actively worked to target and undermine our national security interest.

Iranian technology and rockets have been used to launch thousands of rockets further into Israel, placing the majority of the country at risk. And the regime's financial support has allowed Hamas to continue to resupply itself after its stockpiles run low or are destroyed by Israel. Yet for all that we know of the relationship between Iran and these terrorist groups, the administration has ignored this all in its pursuit of its weak nuclear deal with Iran.

In fact, the Iranian regime's support for terror, its ballistic missile program, or its human rights record, aren't even on the table in these negotiations. So while we continue to give away the store, we strengthen and legitimize Iran and embolden other actors who see just how naive we truly are being to this threat.

We saw how well this approach worked with North Korea during those nuclear negotiations, and I was one of the first who admonished the Bush administration for its mistake to take North Korea off the list of state sponsor of terrorism and for the terrible example that it set for future nuclear talks with this rogue regime.

While North Korea continues to circumvent and violate U.N. National Security Council resolutions, like the incident with the North Korean flag vessel and Cuban weapons, or the reports that Pyongyang is seeking to conclude an arms deal with Hamas, it couldn't be any clearer that it deserves to be redesignated as a state sponsor of terrorism country now.

Some of our allies no longer trust us, and our enemies no longer fear us. If we don't take immediate and decisive action against those nations that support terror and undermine our national security, especially those that are supposed allies, then we put our interest and our citizens at greater risk.

We cannot allow this support for terrorism to continue. We must cut off the funds that go to Hamas and other terror groups. Only then can we begin to take down those terrorist groups and counter their radical ideologies. It all starts with the ideology. But like a flame without air, these radical ideologies, without money and support, will die out.

I am pleased to turn to my ranking member, my good friend, Congressman Ted Deutch, for his opening statement.

Mr. DEUTCH. Thank you very much, Chairman Ros-Lehtinen. I would first like to express how proud I am of what this committee and the full House was able to achieve in a bipartisan manner during this summer when Hamas waged war against Israel. We passed a resolution that I co-introduced with you, Madam Chairman, to denounce Hamas' use of human shields as a gross violation of international humanitarian law and a heinous disregard of the basic human rights of the people of Gaza.

We passed another resolution with 166 of our colleagues signing on as co-sponsors making clear to Hamas and the rest of the world that the United States stands firmly and steadfastly with Israel and will support that country as it exercises its right to defend itself from rocket attacks and other terrorist threats.

And I join with many of my colleagues to deliver a message to the U.N. High Commissioner for Human Rights exposing their concentrated focus on Israel rather than Hamas, the terrorist group willing to sacrifice thousands of innocent lives and endanger millions more. All of these actions and plenty more send a clear sign to the world that Congress stands together in support of Israel's security and will forcibly respond to terrorists that threaten it. So I would like to thank my colleagues.

As the cease fire and the conflict between Israel and Gaza has taken hold, we have got to face the challenge of addressing this network of support for Hamas. The simple conclusion that we can reach is that Turkey, Qatar, and Iran all played varying roles in supporting Hamas, whether financially, militarily, politically, or a combination.

These countries stood with Hamas as it encouraged families to remain in buildings as human shields, despite repeated warnings to leave by these Israeli military. These countries stood with Hamas as it spent millions and millions of dollars, not on the welfare of the Palestinian people but on tunnels for terrorizing Israeli communities.

These countries stood with Hamas as it shot thousands of rockets into Israel indiscriminately and targeted urban areas full of civilians. These are despicable acts that were permitted to occur with the continued support from this network. And as I stated before, Congress took appropriate measures to condemn these actions, and I believe that the condemnation can be extended back to Hamas' benefactors.

However, the issue becomes more complicated when you began to zoom out and try to understand the larger regional implications of the conflict and of this terrorist support network. This is where it gets particularly complicated, especially in the context of the Syrian conflict, a calamity that is in desperate need of the world's attention.

The response to the United States thus far has been mostly humanitarian, with some military support to vetted opposition groups. But a great deal of our on-the-ground involvement in Syria is to Syrians inside the country that comes through its northern neighbor, Turkey. It is with cooperation with the Turkish Government that we and other humanitarian partners are able to continue to use their routes into the country.

These are helpful measures that we need to deliver essential aid to millions of Syrians internally displaced and without access to basic supplies or food. The country has also taken in—Turkey, taken in over 800,000 Syrian refugees fleeing death and destruction.

Turkey is also in a position to play a large role in combating ISIL. The threat to the Turks is very tangible. The group is active not far from the Turkish border. Turkey, a NATO ally, may soon have to deal with ISIL not as a threat to the stability of neighboring countries but to the direct security of that nation itself.

The state has begun to take measures to restrict funds and foreign fighters flowing into Syria and is working to reduce the fuel smuggling out of Syria that helps in part to fund ISIL's campaigns. Turkey has joined in Secretary Kerry's announced coalition of states to combat the growing ISIL threat in Syria and Iraq.

However, we cannot turn away from the country's actions during the Hamas-Israel conflict. Turkey not only stood at the side of Hamas, but then Prime Minister Erdogan made egregious and wildly offensive accusations at Israel, comparing Israeli actions to those of Hitler and the Nazis. These statements make it abundantly clear that now President Erdogan and other Turkish leaders have fully embraced this policy of giving support and political cover to Hamas.

So while complex conflicts like this require a careful approach when dealing with our partners in the region, our policy has to remain explicitly clear toward Iran. Hamas' military capacity, including arms, rockets, methods of combat, and general funding, is largely provided by Iran. Repeatedly, the Israelis have intercepted shipments of Iranian arms en route to the Gaza strip. Most recently in March of this year Israelis intercepted the Klos C ship carrying 40 M302 missiles, 181 mortars, 400,000 guns. These are weapons that would have undoubtedly been used against Israel.

We must remember that Hamas was able to reach Tel-Aviv, Jerusalem, and other heavily populated civilian centers largely due to the advanced rockets provided for or funded by Iran. Let me be clear: Any mutual interest that the United States and Iran might have, such as in combating the ISIL threat, will not distract us from our condemnation of Iran's sponsorship of terrorism and our tough stance during negotiations of their nuclear program, nor will it detract from the necessity of preventing a nuclear armed Iran.

We are just now moving away from a turbulent summer during which Israel faced significant threats from a terrorist group right on its border. Countries whose funds, resources, political clout, and vocal public endorsement were used to help Hamas fire rockets into civilian areas, build tunnels, and inflicting pain on innocent families are in some ways implicated for these same crimes.

With things changing every day in the region, requiring new calculations and new strategies, it is important that the United States continue to make decisions based on our national security interest and those of our allies.

I look forward to hearing the testimony of our witnesses today to explain not only the foundation of this network of support for Hamas but the true motivations and interests of these countries and how this information can be used to help shape effective policy decisions here, and I yield back.

Thank you, Madam Chair.

Ms. ROS-LEHTINEN. Thank you very much, Mr. Deutch.

And now I am pleased to recognize Mr. Poe, because we are doing a joint subcommittee hearing. He is the chairman of our Subcommittee on Terrorism. Judge Poe.

Mr. POE. I thank the chair. Hamas is a brutal terrorist organization. They are not a state. They are an international criminal organization that preaches hate and practices murder. The Hamas bigoted charter states, ''The day of judgment will not come until Muslims fight Jews and kill them. And even stones and trees will call on Muslims to come and kill the Jews.''

Specifically, the charter also calls for the annihilation and destruction of Israel. ''Israel will exist and will continue to exist until Islam will obliterate it, just as it obliterated others before it.''

And Hamas has not revised this charter. It has not disavowed parts of it at all. It still refuses to recognize Israel's right to exist and still calls for the killing of Jews. In 2006, Hamas senior leader Mahad Al-Zahra said that the group ''will not change a single word of this covenant.'' Hamas invented the tactic of suicide bombing that murdered many Israelis.

In April 1993, Syria's peace negotiations between Israel and the Palestinian leadership were underway. Hamas hates peace, so it had an operative named Tamom Nablusi drive a van into a parked bus and detonate it. This was the first-ever suicide bombing and it killed a Palestinian and wounded eight Israeli soldiers. Since then, Hamas has been responsible for the murder of hundreds— hundreds of innocent Israelis.

Hamas does not care about the lives or needs of the Palestinians either. As millions of Palestinians suffer from unemployment and the lack of basic services, Hamas spends money of its ill-gotten gain on tunnels and rockets from Iran designated to kill, yes, Israelis. It cannot govern and it will only drag Palestinians further into despair.

During Protective Edge, Israel's most recent operation against Hamas, the Israelis, in defense of their nation, destroyed or intercepted a majority of Hamas' rocket supply, maybe as many as 8,000 rockets. The U.N. and the world media faulted Israel for this war. They got it wrong. Hamas is a foreign terrorist organization. It is not a state. Israel acted in self-defense, and all countries have the sovereign right to do it. And we should make it clear that the United States supports Israel in this endeavor.

Destroying rockets will not get rid of this problem, however. Hamas gets shipments of rockets from Iran and makes rockets from dual use material thanks to technology and know-how from Iran. It is only a matter of time before they reload and start firing those offensive rockets again.

To stop Hamas, we must go after its finances and its suppliers, and there is plenty of evidence that Qatar and NATO partner Turkey, in addition to Iran, are the main backers of Hamas. Qatar and Turkey have pledged public and financial support to the tune of hundreds of millions of dollars.

Khaled Meshaal, the leader of Hamas, lives comfortably in Qatar while the Palestinians go hungry. He lives along with a number of other senior commanders. In Turkey, the leader of a Hamas military wing, Qassam Brigades, also lives freely. The actions of Qatar and Turkey have inflamed relations with friendly Sunni Arab countries in the region, like Jordan, the UAE, and the Saudis.

Qatar and Turkey should be held accountable for their actions, not just in Gaza with Hamas, but their support for other Sunni extremist groups. The United States must get tough with Qatar while looking at alternatives for our military bases in Qatar.

Terrorist organizations, including Hamas, use Qatar as a financial clearinghouse. Despite years of U.S. Government urging Qatar to crack down, things have just gotten worse. In Turkey, Erdogan, our Erdogan regime must cut ties with Hamas and the Muslim Brotherhood or there is going to be consequences. There are all sorts of illicit financial transactions being processed through Turkey, including Iranian activity designed to skirt sanctions. No one should be surprised.

It is time for the United States Government to wake up and see the Middle East for what it is and what it has become, not what we would just like it to be. If Hamas is going to be defeated, its money flow has to stop. We cannot stop Hamas' finances by ourselves. We need countries in the region to work with us. If we want peace for the United States and peace for our ally, Israel, we must make our message clear. If you help finance Hamas, there will be significant consequences, and they will be unpleasant.

I hope Qatar and Turkey are listening. No more filthy lucre to finance Hamas. And that is just the way it is.

I will yield back.

Ms. ROS-LEHTINEN. Thank you so much, Judge Poe.

Try to top that, Mr. Sherman, ranking member of Terrorism Subcommittee.

Mr. SHERMAN. Thank the chairman and my fellow ranking member for holding these hearings. It is important that we identify the benefactors of Hamas, so that we can effectively deny it material and political support. Keep in mind, Hamas' strategy is to create as many civilian casualties as possible on both sides. That is why its rocket attacks are designed to create as many civilian casualties in Israel, and then it uses as its chief political weapon the fact that there are civilian casualties among the Palestinians. Virtually every rocket it sends is a war crime, since its purpose is to kill civilians.

The Israelis admirably have sought to minimize civilian casualties, and they have incurred losses as a result. If Israel had used bunker buster bombs to destroy tunnels, there would have been fewer Israeli casualties, and a lot more Palestinian civilians would have died. Instead, Israel sent in its ground forces, and it is that decision that caused virtually all of Israel's casualties in the most recent war.

We have got to avoid the body bag count method of moral analysis. We cannot assume that whichever side loses the most civilians has morality on its side. By that analysis, Eisenhower is a war criminal, since there are far more German deaths, civilian and military, than there were American.

We know that Hamas has instigated the current conflict by kidnapping the three teenagers and firing rockets. We know that the purpose of the rockets it sent was to kill as many Israeli civilians as possible. For example, an Israeli child is killed by these rockets. It is not a tragic mistake for Hamas; it is a cause of celebration.

The Iron Dome did much not only to save Israeli civilians but to save Palestinian civilians that would have died had Israel engaged in an even more robust response, which would have been necessary had there been more Israeli civilian casualties.

So who are Hamas' benefactors? We have heard them from the other opening statements. They are Qatar and Turkey and Iran. Iran has played a major role. There was a falling out in 2001 over Hamas siding with the anti-Assad forces in Syria. That has been patched up to some degree. But Iran is so preoccupied with other events involving Shiites from Lebanon to Iraq that it has reduced its support for Hamas for both political and economic reasons.

Qatar—it has been described as 300 families and a TV station, 300 families, a TV station, and a ton of petro dollars. Qatar often takes the role of trying to be close with every side of every conflict in the Middle East. They are buying $11 billion worth of our weapons, and they host the forward base of CENTCOM, the al Udeid Air Base.

Their defense depends on us. We took the position during the first Gulf War that we would not allow small oil-rich kingdoms or sheikdoms to be wiped off the map. I don't know if they should assume, given their policies, that that Kuwait Rule applies to Qatar.

Turkey is providing substantial political support and economic support. $300 million was set aside for the Hamas government in 2011, and Hamas allows its ''charities'' to fund Hamas directly. Pending weapons sales, military-to-military relations, economic sanctions, and the use of financial sanctions and blacklists for charitable organizations are all important levers.

We have to focus not only on what the Governments of Turkey and Qatar do, but what they allow their wealthy citizens to do through trusts and foundations. And I look forward to our witnesses' testimony and their recommendations on how to attack this problem.

I yield back.

Ms. ROS-LEHTINEN. You did a very good job, Mr. Sherman.

Mr. SHERMAN. Well, you set a high standard. You compared me to the gentleman from Texas.

Ms. ROS-LEHTINEN. I know. After Judge Poe, that is tough.

I will now be proud to recognize members for their 1-minute opening statements, and we will just go by the board that is right in front of your screen. Mr. Chabot of Ohio, our subcommittee chair.

Mr. CHABOT. Thank you, Madam Chair and Chairman Poe, for holding this important hearing to take a look at the links between Hamas and its supporters. Hamas required billions of dollars and considerable access to weapons and technology to carry on the nearly 2-month-long war against Israel.

I, and I believe many of my colleagues, believe that the source of Hamas' weapons and financial resources warrants considerable scrutiny. Although the conflict has quieted down for now, I am deeply concerned about the support provided to Hamas by a handful of global actors, despite Hamas' reprehensible policy of maximizing civilian casualties.

And as chairman of the Asia-Pacific Subcommittee, I continue to be concerned about North Korea's support for Hamas and other terrorist groups. I want to, again, thank both of you for holding this hearing, as well as our ranking members, and I yield back the balance of my time.

Ms. ROS-LEHTINEN. Thank you, sir.

Mr. Connolly of Virginia.

Mr. CONNOLLY. Thank you, Madam Chairman. I think there are four things that are pretty clear about Hamas and the situation in Gaza. One, Hamas must abjure its own charter and radically alter its behavior if it is ever going to have any respectable place at the international table.

Secondly, its benefactors need to cut off its financial pipeline right now. Thirdly, the recent violence in the Gaza does show that there is no substitute for a long-term committed, sustained peace process between Israel and its Palestinian neighbors. And, fourth, the United States must remain engaged if we are ever going to end the cycle of violence in the Middle East.

Thank you, Madam Chairman.

Ms. ROS-LEHTINEN. Thank you, sir.

Mr. Brooks.

Mr. BROOKS. Thank you, Madam Chairman. I defer my time so that we can hear the witnesses.

Ms. ROS-LEHTINEN. Mr. Kennedy.

Mr. KENNEDY. Thank you, Madam Chairman. And I want to thank the witnesses for their testimony and look forward to hearing what you have to say. I echo the sentiments from our colleagues, very much looking forward to any suggestions you might have about how we can crack down on the financing of Hamas and their sources of income.

And, secondly, what we can try to do to build up civil society there to erode support for Hamas in the long term as well. This became such a challenge because they were able to win an election. They were able to provide government services and give an explanation to the residents of Gaza as to why they should be representing them in government.

What suggestions do you have for us about how we can make that case more explicit as to why that is not so?

Thank you.

Ms. ROS-LEHTINEN. Thank you, sir.

Mr. Perry.

Mr. PERRY. Thanks, Madam Chair. I am just going to reserve time for the witnesses.

Thank you.

Ms. ROS-LEHTINEN. Mr. Higgins.

Mr. HIGGINS. Thank you, Madam Chair. Having visited Gaza many times, you are struck with the great potential of that region located along the Mediterranean, a population of less than 2 million, really a beautiful place in the sun potentially, but for the fact that Hamas is in control.

And we see that time and again Hamas is not concerned about the death and destruction that happens in Gaza with some 2,100 lives, 72 percent of whom are civilians. Rather, they seek to exploit Palestinian pain and suffering, and these are the conditions they seek to exploit, not conditions that they seek to end.

So I look forward to today's discussion with our witnesses, and with that I will yield back.

Ms. ROS-LEHTINEN. Mr. Clawson.

Mr. CLAWSON. After watching thousands of rockets fired into Gaza—into Israel from Gaza in the last 50-day war, it is clear that Gaza must be demilitarized. The first step of course is what some of my colleagues have already mentioned so clearly, and that is defunding. And the best way to do that is to follow the money.

I am curious about what banking institutions are involved and how the transactions can even happen. It is not easy to move money across borders, in the Western world in particular. So that is my first question that you all might want to answer for us. And what countries are funneling that money? A lot of that has already been mentioned.

So let us follow the money here today, see what allies of ours are involved, and let us see if we can cut the tap off.

Thank you.

Ms. ROS-LEHTINEN. Thank you, sir.

Mr. Schneider.

Mr. SCHNEIDER. Thank you, Madam Chairman, and thank you again for calling this important hearing. I would also like to echo the words of the ranking member on the hard and good work that this committee, the full committee, did over the summer during the war and look forward to continuing to do that.

As far as today's hearing, I think it is crucial that we have the opportunity to more deeply understand the support, the vast support network, that is funding and allowing Hamas to carry out its nefarious activities. I think it is crucial that we look for ways to change that network or influence and change the dynamics, so Hamas does come and continue to face the pressures, to alter their strategies and change their calculations.

I would also like to hear from the witnesses today a little more in depth about the vast wealth accumulated by many of the leaders of Hamas while many of the people in Gaza are suffering and living in absolute poverty. But this is a crucial issue, and I am grateful that the committee is having this hearing.

Thank you.

Ms. ROS-LEHTINEN. Thank you, Mr. Schneider.

Mr. Duffy.

Mr. DUFFY. I will reserve my time, Madam Chair.

Ms. ROS-LEHTINEN. Mr. Lowenthal.

Mr. LOWENTHAL. I yield.

Ms. ROS-LEHTINEN. Thank you.

Mr. DeSantis.

Mr. DESANTIS. Thank you, Madam Chairwoman. Thank you for calling this hearing. It is interesting to me we have heard a lot of members, I think correctly, talk about Turkey's role in funding Hamas, talking about Qatar's role, and we see these guys as the usual suspects for what is going on with ISIS, too. You have jihadists pouring into Syria. Where are they getting there from? They are getting there through Turkey.

And so you have a President in Turkey who has aligned his country firmly on the side of the Muslim Brotherhood, and I would say that global jihad is just somebody who is supposed to be a part of NATO. So I think this cries out for more examination. And, of course, Qatar to continue to fund Sunni supremacism throughout the region, it is very much antagonistic to our interest and to the interest of our allies such as Israel.

So thank you, Madam Chairwoman. I yield back.

Ms. ROS-LEHTINEN. Thank you.

Mr. Castro yields back. So Mr. Meadows is recognized.

Mr. MEADOWS. I would just like to hear from our witnesses the correlation between Hamas' funding now and how that parallels what we have seen with Hezbollah using charitable organizations, money laundering, et cetera, to fund much of their activity. It seems like the nexus there is indeed Iran, and I would love for you to comment on that.

And I will yield back, Madam Chair.

Ms. ROS-LEHTINEN. Thank you, sir.

Dr. Yoho.

Mr. YOHO. Thank you, Madam Chair. I would like to hear from you guys, as we go through this, recommendings on how we can change the dynamics over there. As Mr. Sherman brought out, Hamas' strategy is to create as many civilian casualties as possible. And with the foreign aid that we give to the Palestinian Authority of $500 million a year, and in their own Resolution 21 and 23 they reward terrorists for creating crimes of terror and killing people, Israeli citizens and American citizens, they pay them a monthly stipend.

I want to hear your recommendations on removing that and if that is—if you guys think that is a plausible thing that we should do. We have put in a resolution to get rid of that, and I would like to hear your comments.

Thank you.

Ms. ROS-LEHTINEN. Thank you, sir.

Mr. Cook. Thank you.

Mr. Rohrabacher.

Mr. ROHRABACHER. Thank you. I would just like to associate my-self with the——

Ms. ROS-LEHTINEN. Microphone.

Mr. ROHRABACHER. Yes. Hello. I would like to associate myself with the profound and passionate remarks of Judge Poe.

Mr. SHERMAN. Especially that filthy lucre. I liked that, Judge Poe.

Ms. ROS-LEHTINEN. And to wrap up, Mr. Weber.

Mr. WEBER. Let us go.

Ms. ROS-LEHTINEN. All right. Thank you very much. Thank you to all of our members for a wonderful attendance. We should give out cookies next week, Eddy. This is wonderful. And Mr. Deutch came on time, early even. What? So pretty good. Working on being a Senator, we hear.

So we are so pleased to welcome back to our subcommittee Dr. Jonathan Schanzer, who is vice president for research for the Foundation for Defense of Democracies. Prior to this, Dr. Schanzer served as a counterterrorism analyst at the U.S. Department of the Treasury where he took part in the designation of numerous terrorism financiers.

Thank you so much.

We will then hear from Mr. Avi Jorisch. Mr. Jorisch is a senior fellow for counterterrorism at the American Foreign Policy Council. Prior to this, Mr. Jorisch also served at the Department of the Treasury as a policy advisor in the Office of Terrorism and Financial Intelligence, as well as a liaison to the Department of Homeland Security and as a terrorism consultant for the Department of Defense. Welcome.

And last, but certainly not least, we would like to welcome Dr. Steven Cook. Dr. Cook comes to us from the Council of Foreign Relations where he is a senior fellow for Middle Eastern studies. Prior to this, Dr. Cook was a research fellow at the Brookings Institute and Washington Institute for Near East Policy.

Thank you so much. We are so pleased with our distinguished panel. As I said, your prepared statements have already been made part of the record, and we will first hear from Dr. Schanzer. Thank you.

STATEMENT OF JONATHAN SCHANZER, PH.D., VICE PRESIDENT FOR RESEARCH, FOUNDATION FOR DEFENSE OF DEMOCRACIES

Mr. SCHANZER. Chairman Ros-Lehtinen, Chairman Poe, Ranking Member Deutch, Ranking Member Sherman, and distinguished members of these two subcommittees, thank you for the opportunity to testify today about Hamas finance.

I should note up front that Egypt, under the Muslim Brotherhood regime of Mohamed Morsi, previously served as a major hub of Hamas finance. But since the ouster of Morsi by Abdel Fattah al-Sisi, the regime in Egypt has delivered a blow to Hamas finance by shutting down some 1,700 smuggling tunnels. This has deprived Hamas of the opportunity to tax its people on smuggled goods and has encumbered the group's ability to transfer cash to its own coffers.

With Egypt now under control, there are four other jurisdictions that contribute to Hamas' estimated $1 billion annual budget, and those countries are Qatar, Turkey, Iran, and Sudan. Qatar is currently Hamas' ATM. In the words of Treasury Undersecretary David Cohen, Qatar has "for many years openly financed Hamas." The previous Emir pledged $400 million to Hamas in 2012. Qatar is also the home of many Hamas figures, including Hamas popular leader Khaled Meshaal. During my trip to Doha last year, one expatriate quipped to me that residents of Doha catch sight of Meshaal the way New Yorkers talk of seeing Woody Allen.

Qatar was Hamas' greatest advocate during the recent Gaza war, and Doha doesn't stop there. It supports many other terrorist groups, as has already been mentioned, yet we call Qatar an ally and maintain our largest air base in the Middle East on Qatari soil.

Turkey is another such "frenemy." A NATO ally, Turkey has in recent years become a haven for at least a dozen Hamas figures, including the founder of Hamas's military wing in the West Bank. His name is Saleh al-Arouri. Arouri recently made headlines when he announced that Hamas killed the three Israeli teens in the West Bank in June. Tellingly, he made this announcement in the presence of Turkey's Deputy Prime Minister, who was there in the audience.

Reports also suggest that Turkey may have pledged $300 million to Hamas several years ago. But Turkey's support to terror doesn't end there. Turkey has maintained a dangerous border policy that has contributed to the rise of ISIS. Ankara has also helped Iran, another Hamas patron, evade sanctions.

Iran's support to Hamas is a complicated story. While it was once the group's top patron, Iran's support to Hamas has declined over disagreements about the serious civil war. However, it is clear that strong military ties continue. The long-range rockets fired by Hamas in the recent war, M302s, were furnished by Iran. Many of the smaller and indigenously produced rockets in Gaza are the result of Iranian technical assistance. More broadly, Hamas' guerilla capabilities have improved markedly over the years thanks to Iranian arms and training.

Sudan, meanwhile, plays a significant role in the smuggling of larger rockets to Hamas, and this does not get a lot of attention. Iran ships these rockets by sea, and they often arrive in Port Sudan. From there, they are smuggled up through Egypt and across the Sinai Peninsula. Sudan has also stored Iranian rockets for Hamas. Notably, Israel bombed the Khartoum warehouse full of Fajr 5 rockets in October 2012.

Madam and Mr. Chairman, I now offer these recommendations to Congress for consideration.

Number one, support Egypt's efforts to deter Hamas finance. They are doing more than was expected of them. They deserve our assistance in this regard.

Number two, pressure Qatar to freeze Hamas assets and expel Khaled Meshaal, along with Hamas leaders.

Number three, pressure Turkey to freeze Hamas assets and expel Saleh al-Arouri, along with Hamas leaders.

Number four, Treasury should designate individuals and entities in both Qatar and Turkey that are involved in terrorism finance.

Five, Congress should consider putting a hold on U.S. military sales to Qatar and Turkey until Hamas finance is addressed.

Number six, conduct hearings and demand intelligence assessments of Qatar and Turkey. Both countries are involved in a lot more illicit financial activity than merely supporting Hamas.

Seven, conduct an assessment by the GAO or the Pentagon on what it would take to move the al Udeid Air Base out of Qatar. It is difficult to justify our presence there while Qatar supports Hamas and other terrorist groups.

Number eight, work with our defense and intelligence agencies to use both carrots and sticks to convince Qatar and Turkey to halt their support to Hamas.

Number nine, consider ways to address the problem of terrorism finance through the JPOA nuclear talks with Iran.

Number ten, keep the pressure on Iran through Treasury's terrorism sanctions. More of those are needed always.

And, finally, we must work with regional partners to block weapons shipments to Port Sudan.

On behalf of the Foundation for Defense of Democracies, I thank you for inviting me to testify today, and I look forward to your questions.

Thank you.

[The prepared statement of Mr. Schanzer follows:]

Congressional Testimony

Hamas's Benefactors:
A Network of Terror

Jonathan Schanzer
Vice President for Research
Foundation for Defense of Democracies

Hearing before the
House Committee on Foreign Affairs
Subcommittee on the Middle East and North Africa
Subcommittee on Terrorism, Nonproliferation, and Trade

Washington, DC
September 9, 2014

DEFENSE OF DEMOCRACIES   1726 M Street NW • Suite 700 • Washington, DC 20036

Chairman Ros-Lehtinen, Chairman Poe, Ranking Member Deutch, Ranking Member Sherman, and distinguished members of these subcommittees, on behalf of the Foundation for Defense of Democracies, I thank you for the opportunity to discuss with you today the state sponsors of the Palestinian terrorist group Hamas.

Hamas poses many challenges in the Middle East. It is one of the primary impediments to peace between Israel and the Palestinians. Its violent attacks have killed hundreds of Israelis over the years, prompted wars, and derailed diplomacy. The group also poses a political and military challenge to the Palestinian Authority (PA), which is admittedly not an ideal partner for the United States or Israel, but is currently the best of a bad lot. It is for these reasons that Hamas's finances need to be countered.

Tracking Hamas's finances is complicated. The movement maintains a complex network of charities and front companies across the Middle East and even here in the United States. The way that funds move from one entity to another is typically shrouded from the public eye. But in some cases, particularly when states are involved, Hamas's financial activities have been exposed. In this testimony, I endeavor to identify the jurisdictions where financial, military, and material support to Hamas is prevalent. I also identify members of Hamas abroad who may hold significant funds in their accounts. I will conclude with several recommendations of possible policy options for the United States Congress and the Administration.

Steps Taken

Before addressing some the current challenges, it is worth briefly reviewing some of Washington's successes in battling Hamas finance. The U.S. Treasury has done an admirable job in encumbering Hamas's ability to raise and move money over the last 20 years.

It began in the Clinton administration in 1995, when the president declared Hamas to be a designated terrorist organization. This was followed by the designation of Hamas in 1997 as a Foreign Terrorist Organization. After the September 11 attacks, Hamas was designated by the Treasury as a specially designated global terrorist (SDGT) entity.[1] The Treasury also scored a major win against Hamas finance here in the United States with the designation of the Holy Land Foundation for Relief and Development. Mousa Abu Marzook, a long-standing senior Hamas figure, was one of its board members.[2] The Foundation is still fighting legal battles.[3]

In 2003, Treasury designated a raft of senior Hamas figures, including: Khaled Meshal (Politburo chief), Imad al-Alami (envoy to Iran and Syria), Osama Hamdan (Lebanon envoy), Mousa Abu Marzook (Egypt-based politburo), Ahmed Yassin (Hamas founder, assassinated 2004), and Abdel Aziz Rantisi (Yassin's successor, assassinated 2004). Treasury in 2003 also

---

[1] "Protecting Charitable Organizations: Additional Background Information on Charities Designated Under Executive Order 13224," *U.S. Department of the Treasury Website*, accessed September 4, 2014. (http://www.treasury.gov/resource-center/terrorist-illicit-finance/Pages/protecting-charities_execorder_13224-c.aspx)

[2] "הטייקונים של חמאס: ח'אלד משעל שווה 2-5 מיליארד דולר, סגנו אבו-מרזוק שווה 2-3 מיליארד דולר," *Globes* (Israel), July 24, 2014. (http://www.globes.co.il/news/article.aspx?did=1000957870)

[3] Terry Baynes, "Muslim Charity Leaders Lose Appeal in Hamas Case," *Reuters*, December 7, 2011. (http://www.reuters.com/article/2011/12/08/us-crime-hamas-idUSTRE7B707L20111208)

targeted five Hamas charities: Commite de Bienfaisance et de Secours aux Palestiniens (France), The Association de Secours Palestinien (Switzerland), The Palestinian Relief and Development Fund also known as Interpal (U.K.), The Palestinian Association in Austria, and the Sanabil Association for Relief and Development (Lebanon).[4]

Following Hamas's electoral victory in 2006, Treasury authorized U.S. financial institutions to reject all transactions with members of the Palestinian Legislative Council elected on the Hamas party slate.[5] The list of individuals included more than 100 Hamas members not previously designated, including prominent Hamas officials, such as Ismail Haniyeh and Mahmoud al-Zahar.[6] Treasury also took action against KindHearts, an NGO based out of Ohio, for allegedly financing Hamas.[7]

In 2007, Treasury designated al-Salah Society based in the Palestinian Territories. The charity was accused of financing schools, stores, and the purchase of land for Hamas members. It also employed a number of members of the Izz al-Din al-Qassam Brigades, the armed wing of Hamas.[8] Al-Salah Society was also believed to have a connection to Hamas accounts at Arab Bank – the defendant in a terrorism finance case currently being litigated.[9]

Treasury followed up in 2009 with the designation of an umbrella organization that controlled al-Salah, known as the Union of Good or *Ittilaf al-Kheir*. The group was created by Hamas leadership in late 2000 in order to transfer funds raised by affiliates for Hamas-managed projects in the West Bank and Gaza. The Union of Good employed a number of Qassam Brigades members.[10] The Union also included the Turkish flotilla, the IHH, which has very close ties to Hamas (and will be discussed below).

In 2010, Treasury targeted the Islamic National Bank (INB) of Gaza, as well as Hamas's al-Aqsa TV. Hamas opened INB in Gaza City in 2009 without approval from the Palestinian Monetary Authority and PA. Hamas's finance office in Gaza subsequently wired INB €1.1 million, which then was paid to members of the Qassam Brigades. Al-Aqsa TV, a vitriolic tool of incitement, was designated as a terrorist entity after the Hamas leadership in Damascus allocated hundreds of thousands of dollars for the station's budget.[11]

---

[4] U.S. Department of the Treasury, Office of Foreign Assets Control, "What You Need to Know About U.S. Sanctions," August 29, 2014. (http://www.treasury.gov/resource-center/sanctions/programs/documents/terror.pdf)
[5] U.S. Department of the Treasury, Press Release, "Palestinian Legislative Council (PLC) List," April 12, 2006. (http://www.treasury.gov/resource-center/sanctions/Terrorism-Proliferation-Narcotics/Pages/index.aspx)
[6] U.S. Department of the Treasury, Press Release, "NS-PLC List," April 12, 2006. (http://www.treasury.gov/resource-center/sanctions/Programs/Documents/plc_list.pdf)
[7] U.S. Department of the Treasury, Press Release, "Treasury Freezes Assets of Organization Tied to Hamas," February 19, 2006. (http://www.treasury.gov/press-center/press-releases/Pages/js4058.aspx)
[8] U.S. Department of the Treasury, Press Release, "Treasury Designates Al-Salah Society Key Support Node for Hamas," August 7, 2007. (http://www.treasury.gov/press-center/press-releases/Pages/hp531.aspx)
[9] "Bank Accounts For Hamas-Controlled Organizations," *Osen LLC*, accessed September 4, 2014. (http://www.osenlaw.com/content/bank-accounts-hamas-controlled-organizations)
[10] U.S. Department of the Treasury, Press Release, "Union of Good," February 3, 2009. (http://www.treasury.gov/resource-center/terrorist-illicit-finance/Pages/protecting-union-of-good.aspx)
[11] U.S. Department of the Treasury, Press Release, "Treasury Designates Gaza-Based Business, Television Station for Hamas Ties," March 18, 2010. (http://www.treasury.gov/press-center/press-releases/Pages/tg594.aspx)

In 2012, Treasury targeted Al-Waqfiya and Al-Quds Charities (Lebanon). Both organizations raise money for programs and projects in the Palestinian Territories for Hamas. Al-Waqfiya is a member of the Union of Good.[12]

Egypt and the Collapse of the Syria-Iran Axis

Despite these efforts, Hamas continued to finance itself with relative ease. But Hamas's fortunes in recent years have taken a significant hit.

For one, the downfall of the Muslim Brotherhood government in Egypt was a blow to Hamas finance and the movement's de facto government in the Gaza Strip. Egypt under Mohammed Morsi was a major external base of Hamas operations. One senior Israeli official once called it the "back office of Hamas." The same official indicated to me that elements of the Brotherhood's financial network were bankrolling Hamas, even as Egypt's economy cratered.[13] Egypt was so central to Hamas's operations, the movement held a round of internal elections in the Egyptian capital.[14]

In the weeks after Morsi's ouster, the new regime froze the accounts of least 30 Brotherhood figures,[15] including at least one significant contributor to Hamas's coffers, according to a senior Israeli security official. Although it is possible that some Hamas money remains unfrozen in Egypt, Cairo is still hunting Muslim Brotherhood and Hamas accounts.[16] According to one Israeli report, Cairo-based Hamas leader Mousa Abu Marzook is currently worth $2-$3 billion.[17] Arab media sources put Abu Marzook's net worth at $3 billion.[18] It is unclear whether Cairo has seized these assets or if Marzook is under investigation.

The regime of President Abdel Fattah al-Sisi has also destroyed more than 1,639 subterranean smuggling tunnels connecting Egypt to Gaza.[19] The importance of the destruction of the tunnels cannot be emphasized enough. The crackdown has made bulk cash smuggling—the primary way Hamas's bank accounts can be replenished—exceedingly difficult. Tunnels also augmented Hamas's income over the past decade because Hamas taxed the goods that came through them. The tunnels were first created as a means to smuggle weapons into the coastal enclave, but after Hamas conquered Gaza, prompting Israel to impose a blockade, the tunnels became a key artery for a wide range of goods to keep the economy running. Hamas, as Gaza's de facto rulers,

---

[12] U.S. Department of the Treasury, Press Release, "Treasury Sanctions Two Hamas-Controlled Charities," October 4, 2012. (http://www.treasury.gov/press-center/press-releases/Pages/tg1725.aspx)

[13] Phone interview with senior Israeli official, July 21, 2013.

[14] "Hamas Re-Elects Exiled Leader Meshaal For A New Term: Official," Al-Arabiya (Saudi Arabia), April 2, 2013. (http://english.alarabiya.net/en/2013/04/02/Hamas-re-elects-exiled-leader-Meshaal-for-a-new-term-official.html)

[15] Aya Ibrahim, "Funds Of Qaradawi, 29 Other MB Frozen," The Cairo Post (Egypt), May 13, 2014. (http://thecairopost.com/news/110206/news/funds-of-qaradawi-29-other-mb-frozen)

[16] Interview with Arab diplomat, Washington D.C., September 4, 2014.

[17] "הטייקונים של חמאס: ח'אלד משעל שווה 5-2 מיליארד דולר. סגנו אבו-מרזוק שווה 3-2 מיליארד דולר" Globes (Israel), July 24, 2014. (http://www.globes.co.il/news/article.aspx?did=1000957870)

[18] " مليارديرات "حماس": هنية يملك اربعة مليارات.. ومشعل خمسة.. وابو مرزوق ثلاثة.. والله عيب يا اعلام مصر ان تهبط الى هذا المستوى في " Ra'i al-Youm (United Kingdom), July 26, 2014. حملاتكم التحريضية على قادة يتصدون لابشع عنوان (http://www.raialyoum.com/?p=127306)

[19] "Egypt Army Destroys 13 More Gaza Tunnels," Agence France Presse, July 27, 2014. http://news.yahoo.com/egypt-army-destroys-13-more-gaza-tunnels-093712884.html

reportedly collected at least $365 million in taxes each year from the tunnel trade.[20] During Morsi's presidency, Hamas reportedly charged Gazans nearly eight times the subsidized price of Egyptian fuel being imported into Gaza. It is also believed that the wealth of Hamas leaders—some of whom may even be billionaires—was primarily derived from the 20 percent tax established on products smuggled through the tunnels on the Gaza border with Egypt.[21]

Ala al-Rafati, the Hamas economy minister, last year told Reuters that these anti-tunnel operations cost Hamas $230 million—about one-tenth of Gaza's GDP.[22] And that was before another estimated 900 tunnels were destroyed.

All of this came at a horrendous time for Hamas. Until 2012, the faction relied heavily on Iran and Syria for financial support. But the civil war in Syria prompted Hamas to reconsider this relationship. The Hamas leadership left its longtime base in Damascus after the carnage in Syria became too great. The Sunni Palestinian group could not maintain its credibility among Palestinians if it stood by the Assad regime as it killed Sunnis and Palestinians by the thousands. Before Hamas left Damascus, the group's assets there were estimated at nearly $550 million.[23] But it is unclear if Hamas leaders were able to leave with those funds in hand.

In the end, Iran reportedly cut a significant amount of its funding to Hamas.[24] The relationship between Hamas and Iran is not defunct. Cooperation continues, as noted below. But without as much direct financial support from Iran, Hamas was forced to turn to the Muslim Brotherhood bloc to make ends meet.

Qatar

Qatar appears to have filled much of the void left by Iran. Some of the support it provides is political. During the recent Gaza war between Hamas and Israel, Qatar played a crucial political role for Hamas, pushing a plan designed to benefit the terrorist group above all else. The Qataris angled for a one-sided deal that would have ignored Israel's security concerns, and pushed for Hamas's integration in the global economy.

But Qatar's role is not only a political one. As one Arab diplomat recently told me, "Qatar finances Hamas strongly."[25] In 2006, shortly after the elections that brought Hamas to power, Qatar offered $50 million to what was then a Hamas-dominated Palestinian Authority

[20] David Lev, "IDF: Hamas Makes A Million A Day In 'Taxes' On Smuggled Goods," *Arutz Sheva* (Israel), February 11, 2013. (http://www.israelnationalnews.com/News/News.aspx/165125#.VAnpC_mwJgl)
[21] Doron Peskin, "Hamas Got Rich As Gaza Was Plunged Into Poverty," *YNet News* (Israel), July 15, 2014. (http://www.ynetnews.com/articles/0,7340,L-4543634,00.html)
[22] Nidal al-Mughrabi, "Hamas Reeling From Egyptian Crackdown On Gaza Tunnels," *Aswat Masriya* (Egypt), July 21, 2013. (http://en.aswatmasriya.com/news/view.aspx?id=2c404781-4e17-412e-8e03-7e2804bf7417)
[23] Doron Peskin, "Hamas Got Rich As Gaza Was Plunged Into Poverty," *YNet News* (Israel), July 15, 2014. (http://www.ynetnews.com/articles/0,7340,L-4543634,00.html)
[24] Robert Tait, "Iran Cuts Hamas Funding Over Syria," *The Telegraph* (U.K.), May 31, 2013. (http://www.telegraph.co.uk/news/worldnews/middleeast/palestinianauthority/10091629/Iran-cuts-Hamas-funding-over-Syria.html)
[25] Interview with Arab diplomat, Washington, DC, September 4, 2014.

government.[26] In 2008, Palestinian officials claimed that Qatar provided Hamas with "millions of dollars a month" that was nominally intended for the people of Gaza.[27] In February 2012, Hamas announced that it would sign a deal with Qatar to receive $250 million for reconstruction projects in Gaza, including 5,000 new homes and repairs to 55,000.[28] In August 2012, Qatar was reported to be opening an office in the Gaza Strip to oversee its various construction endeavors in the coastal enclave.[29]

More famously, in October 2012, Qatar's emir pledged $400 million to Hamas during a high-profile visit to Gaza.[30] His was the only visit by a world leader to Gaza after Hamas took it over by force in 2007. While it is still unclear how much of these Qatari funds were delivered, U.S. officials are convinced that Qatar is bankrolling Hamas. In March of this year, David Cohen, Under Secretary for Terrorism and Financial Intelligence, confirmed that "Qatar, a longtime U.S. ally, has for many years openly financed Hamas."[31]

After Hamas and Fatah reached a reconciliation agreement in May 2014, Qatar pledged $60 million to help Hamas pay salaries to its Gaza employees.[32] In July, Doha tried to transfer funds via Jordan's Arab Bank to pay these salaries.[33] Arab Bank, currently battling a lawsuit on charges of financing Hamas, declined to process the payment, reportedly as a result of U.S. pressure.

Qatar is also the home base of Hamas leader Khaled Meshal. Expatriates in Doha speak of Meshal sightings the way New Yorkers talk of seeing Woody Allen. According to Qatar scholar Allen Fromherz, "after Jordan closed the offices of Hamas in 1999, Qatar offered to allow Khaled Meshal and some of his deputies to relocate to Qatar as long as they did not engage in overt political activities." Fromherz noted that Meshal reportedly "regularly shuttle[d] between Doha and Damascus," where Hamas's external leadership maintained its headquarters until 2012.[34] Meshal, it is worth noting, may have parked some of his cash in Qatar. According to a

---

[26] Christopher M. Blanchard, "Qatar: Background and U.S. Relations," *Congressional Research Service*, June 6, 2012, p. 5. (http://www.au.af.mil/au/awc/awcgate/crs/rl31718.pdf)

[27] "Qatar Seen Bankrolling Hamas," *The Washington Times*, March 5, 2008. (http://www.washingtontimes.com/news/2008/mar/05/qatar-seen-bankrolling-hamas/?page=all)

[28] "Hamas, Qatar To Sign 250 Million USD Deal To Rebuild Gaza," *Xinhua* (China), February 26, 2012. (http://news.xinhuanet.com/english/world/2012-02/26/c_131432557.htm)

[29] "Official: Qatar To Open Office To Oversee Gaza Reconstruction," *Ma'an News Agency* (Palestinian Territories), August 27, 2012. (http://www.maannews.net/eng/ViewDetails.aspx?ID=514177)

[30] Jodi Rudoren, "Qatar's Emir Visits Gaza, Pledging $400 Million To Hamas," *The New York Times*, October 23, 2012. (http://www.nytimes.com/2012/10/24/world/middleeast/pledging-400-million-qatari-emir-makes-historic-visit-to-gaza-strip.html?_r=0)

[31] David Cohen, "Remarks of Under Secretary for Terrorism and Financial Intelligence David Cohen Before The Center for a New American Security on 'Confronting New Threats in Terrorist Financing'," *Speech before the Center for a New American Security*, March 4, 2014. (http://www.treasury.gov/press-center/press-releases/Pages/jl2308.aspx)

[32] Patrick Goodenough, "U.S. Selling $11B In Weaponry To Gulf State That Supports Hamas, Syrian Jihadists," *CNS News*, July 16, 2014. (http://www.cnsnews.com/news/article/patrick-goodenough/us-selling-11b-weaponry-gulf-state-supports-hamas-syrian-jihadists)

[33] Elhanan Miller, "US Blocked Qatari Funds Intended For Hamas Employees," *The Times of Israel* (Israel), July 15, 2014. (http://www.timesofisrael.com/us-blocked-qatari-funds-intended-for-hamas-employees/)

[34] Allen Fromherz, *Qatar: A Modern History*, (Washington, DC: Georgetown University Press, 2012), p. 104.

July 2014 report by the Israeli publication *Globes*, Meshal is currently worth $2.6 billion.[35] Arab media sources put Meshal's net worth at somewhere between $2.5 and $5 billion.[36] Companies registered under the names of Meshal's wife, Amal al-Burini, and one of their daughters, are involved in real estate development projects, including a large shopping mall in Qatar.[37] Meshal's money is also reportedly held in Egyptian and Gulf-based banks,[38] as well as in a number of real estate projects in Saudi Arabia, Syria, and Dubai, all registered under different names.[39]

Qatar also plays host to a gaggle of other senior Hamas figures. As part of the 2011 deal for the release of kidnapped Israeli soldier Gilad Shalit, 15 Hamas members released from Israeli prisons were deported to Qatar and are believed to still be operating there.[40] Additionally, upon the departure of the Hamas leadership from Damascus in 2012, a significant Hamas cadre of leaders relocated to Qatar.[41] Izzat al-Rishq is one prominent member of the Hamas Politburo believed to be based in Qatar. He was deported from Jordan in 1999.[42] Hossam Badran, a Hamas Politburo spokesman, is also based in Qatar.[43] Talal Ibrahim Abd al-Rahman Sharim is a member of the Qassam Brigades, also based in Qatar, who reportedly played a recent role in passing money and directives to Hamas cells in the West Bank.[44]

Turkey

Like Qatar, Turkey was a strident supporter of Hamas during the recent conflict. But it may be a significant financial supporter of the terror group, as well. In December 2011, Palestinian news

---

[35] "הטייקונים של חמאס: ח'אלד משעל שווה 5-2 מיליארד דולר, סמו אבו-מרזוק שווה 3-2 מיליארד דולר," *Globes* (Israel), July 24, 2014. (http://www.globes.co.il/news/article.aspx?did=1000957870)

[36] " مليارديرات "حماس": هنية يملك اربعة مليارات.. ومشعل خمسة.. وابو مرزوق ثلاثة.. والله عيب يا اعلام مصر ان تهبط الى هذا المستوى في حملاتكم التحريضية على قادة يتصدون لابشع عدوان," *Ra'i al-Youm* (United Kingdom), July 26, 2014. (http://www.raialyoum.com/?p=127306)

[37] "Hamas Leaders Worth Millions of Dollars From Allegedly Skimming Donations and Extortion: Is Anyone Surprised?" *Inquisitr*, July 18, 2014. (http://www.inquisitr.com/1359383/hamas-leaders-worth-millions-of-dollars-from-allegedly-skimming-donations-and-extortion-is-anyone-surprised-update/)

[38] "הטייקונים של חמאס: ח'אלד משעל שווה 5-2 מיליארד דולר, סמו אבו-מרזוק שווה 3-2 מיליארד דולר," *Globes* (Israel), July 24, 2014. (http://www.globes.co.il/news/article.aspx?did=1000957870)

[39] Doron Peskin. "Hamas Got Rich As Gaza Was Plunged Into Poverty," *YNet News* (Israel), July 15, 2014. (http://www.ynetnews.com/articles/0,7340,L-4543634,00.html)

[40] "مبعدو صفقة تبادل حركة حماس وإسرائيل," *Wafa* (Palestinian Territories), January 10, 2011 (http://www.wafainfo.ps/atemplate.aspx?id=9155)

[41] Fares Akram, "Hamas Leader Abandons Longtime Base In Damascus," *The New York Times*, January 27, 2012. (http://www.nytimes.com/2012/01/28/world/middleeast/khaled-meshal-the-leader-of-hamas-vacates-damascus.html?_r=0)

[42] "السيرة الذاتية للأستاذ عزت الرشق," *The Islamic Resistance Movement Information Office Website*. January 30, 2011. (http://www.hamasinfo.net/ar/default.aspx?xyz=U6Qq7k%2bcOd87MD146m9rUxJEpMO%2bi1s7iQ8HskLemI5S M%2brbC0Fmcp6%2fLmVI5Kd4zuWWY48rKTYegzTa5QxMn6k8OOr%2fufXwrxID%2fIVuLv2H%2bLaGaG8s I97HrF5VU48dQ93LRgqEcwM%3d)

[43] "Mideast Divisions Cloud Gaza Cease-Fire Efforts," *Mashable*. July 19, 2014, (http://mashable.com/2014/07/19/gaza-cease-fire-efforts/); Maram Hussein, "All Options Are On The Table: Hamas Official," *Qatar Tribune* (Qatar), August 6, 2014. (http://www.qatar-tribune.com/viewnews.aspx?n=0927F2AB-E7B6-414F-BB5F-5F893B63DF98&d=20140806)

[44] Yonah Jeremy Bob, "Shin Bet Busts Palestinian Footballer For Meeting With Hamas Terrorist in Qatar," *The Jerusalem Post* (Israel), June 11, 2014. (http://www.jpost.com/Sports/Palestinian-soccer-player-admits-to-meeting-with-Hamas-operative-while-in-Qatar-356003)

sources reported that Recep Tayyip Erdoğan, then prime minister of Turkey, "instructed the Ministry of Finance to allocate $300 million to be sent to Hamas's government in Gaza."[45] Both Turkey and Hamas denied this, but Reuters[46] and the Israeli *Haaretz*[47] published subsequent reports citing this number. It is also unclear how much of this assistance was delivered, if any.

Turkey, meanwhile, has not been shy about the other financial and material support it provides to the Hamas government in Gaza. Turkey has provided funds for schools,[48] hospitals,[49] mosques,[50] and other supplies[51] to the Hamas regime in Gaza, with additional funds that helped Hamas rebuild after its November 2012 war with Israel. More is expected after this most recent conflict. To be sure, these funds may help the population of Gaza, and that should be welcomed. But Turkey's rather politicized support also legitimizes Hamas in the process.

As if this were not troubling enough, there appears to be a flow of unofficial funds from Turkey to Hamas. According to an Egyptian publication, Muslim Brotherhood groups sent several million dollars to Gaza to help assist civilians to build their houses destroyed in the recent war on the strip. According to the report, a financial officer from Hamas named Essam al-Da'alis did not distribute the funds to civilians to build their homes, but rather dispersed the funds to prominent members of the militant group.[52]

There is also concern here in Washington over the charity that was behind the 2010 flotilla to Gaza, which led to clashes on the high seas. In or around 2001, the Humanitarian Relief Foundation (IHH) became part of the Union of Good, the aforementioned umbrella organization chaired by the Qatar-based cleric Sheikh Yusef al-Qaradawi, who is known for encouraging suicide bombings against Israeli civilians.[53] The U.S. Treasury Department has expressed its

---

[45] Saed Bannoura, "Turkey To Grant Hamas $300 Million," *International Middle East Media Center*, December 3, 2011. (www.imemc.org/article/62607)

[46] Nidal al-Mughrabi, "Hamas Quietly Quits Syria as Violence Continues," *Reuters*, January 27, 2012. (www.reuters.com/article/2012/01/27/us-syria-hamas-idUSTRE80Q0QS20120127)

[47] Zvi Bar'el, "Turkey May Provide Hamas With $300 Million In Annual Aid," *Haaretz* (Israel), January 28, 2012. (www.haaretz.com/news/diplomacy-defense/turkey-may-provide-hamas-with-300-million-in-annual-aid-1.409708)

[48] "Gaza Govt Constructs, Refurbishes 50 Security Buildings," *Ma'an News Agency* (Palestinian Territories), January 24, 2012. (www.maannews.net/eng/ViewDetails.aspx?ID=454664)

[49] "Turkey Building Hospital In Gaza Despite Difficulties," *Today's Zaman* (Turkey), July 19, 2011. (www.todayszaman.com/news-250982-turkey-building-hospital-in-gaza-despite-difficulties.html)

[50] "Turkey To Help Rebuild Mosques In Gaza Strip," *Hurriyet Daily News* (Turkey), January 12, 2012. (www.hurriyetdailynews.com/turkey-to-help-rebuild-mosques-in-gaza-strip.aspx?pageID=238&nID=11286&NewsCatID=338%29)

[51] Elad Benari, "Israel Allows Turkish Food Trucks into Gaza," *Arutz Sheva* (Israel), March 7, 2013. (www.israelnationalnews.com/News/News.aspx/165959#.Uml2uPmsbsI)

[52] "غزة ل"الخوان الدولى قدسها التنظيم أموال على استولت "حماس" : "مصدر, *Al-Youm al-Sab'a* (Egypt), August 16, 2014. (http://www.youm7.com/story/2014/8/16/%D9%85%D8%B5%D8%AF%D8%B1__%D8%AD%D9%85%D8%A7%D8%B3_%D8%A7%D8%B3%D8%AA%D9%88%D9%84%D8%AA_%D8%B9%D9%84%D9%89_%D8%A3%D9%85%D9%88%D8%A7%D9%84_%D9%82%D8%AF%D9%85%D9%87%D8%A7_%D8%A7%D9%84%D8%AA%D9%86%D8%B8%D9%8A%D9%85_%D8%A7%D9%84%D8%AF%D9%88%D9%84%D9%89_%D9%84%D9%84%D8%A5%D8%AE%D9%88%D8%A7%D9%86_%D9%84%D9%80%D8%BA/1821885#.VAir5PldW u_)

[53] "The Union of Good – Analysis and Mapping of Terror Funds Network," *Israel Security Agency Website*, accessed September 4, 2014. (www.shabak.gov.il/english/enterrordata/reviews/pages/coalition.en.aspx)

concerns over whether the IHH provided Hamas with material assistance.[54] To date, however, no designation has been issued, and the IHH continues to operate openly in Gaza.[55]

Turkey also serves as the headquarters for the man described as the founder of the West Bank's Izz al-Din al-Qassam Brigades. The Israeli news website *Ynet* reported last year that Saleh al-Arouri "operates out of Turkey, with the backing of the Turkish government."[56] While al-Arouri's activities are generally below the radar, it is believed that he is raising funds for Hamas. Last year, the Israel Security Agency (Shin Bet) announced the arrest of two Palestinians involved in smuggling money for Hamas from Jordan to the West Bank.[57] During their interrogation, the suspects ceded that some of the money was being smuggled on behalf of al-Arouri.[58]

Al-Arouri is also believed to be in charge of Hamas's terrorist operations in the West Bank, despite some claims that he is simply a member of Hamas's political wing.[59] In January, a senior Israeli military official confirmed this when he told *Israel Hayom* that Hamas's recent West Bank operations are "directed from Gaza via Turkey."[60] More recently, in August, the Israelis announced that al-Arouri was at the center of a plot to bring down the Palestinian Authority government of Mahmoud Abbas in the West Bank. Al-Arouri recruited the leader of the operation, according to reports.[61]

Despite all of this, or perhaps because of it, al-Arouri is held in high regard in Turkey. In March 2012, for example, he was part of a Hamas delegation that took part in talks with Turkish officials, including Erdoğan. The following October, al-Arouri joined Hamas politburo chief Khaled Meshal for a high-level meeting with Erdoğan in Ankara.[62] He is also granted freedom of travel abroad for Hamas activities, including to Gaza and for a recent trip to meet the amir of Kuwait.

---

[54] "Treasury Official On Fight Against Terrorist Financing," *Wikileaks*, December 4, 2009. (http://cablegatesearch.net/cable.php?id=09ANKARA1725)

[55] "Filistin-Gazze," *İHH Website*, accessed September 5, 2014. (http://filistin-gazze.ihh.org.tr/)

[56] Alex Fishman, "Leaving Prison, Returning To Terror." *Ynet News* (Israel), October 21, 2013. (www.ynetnews.com/articles/0,7340,L-4443522,00.html)

[57] David Barnett, "Israel Indicts More Palestinian Terror Cells," *The Long War Journal*, April 18, 2013. (www.longwarjournal.org/threat-matrix/archives/2013/04/israel_indicts_more_palestinia.php)

[58] "מעורבות פעיל ששוחרר ב"עסקת שליט" בהברות טרור," *Israel Security Agency* (Israel), accessed July 16, 2013. (www.shabak.gov.il/publications/publications/Pages/shotef170413.aspx)

[59] "Haniych in Cairo Today, Abu Marzouk Official In Charge Of The Media," *Al Hayat* (Egypt), April 24, 2013. (http://alhayat.com/Details/506404)

[60] Yoav Limor. "'There Is No Intifada'," *Israel Hayom* (Israel), January 10, 2014. (www.israelhayom.com/site/newsletter_article.php?id=14651)

[61] "Israel Says It Foiled Hamas Plan For Massive Attacks On Israel, Coup Against PA," *Times of Israel* (Israel), August 18, 2014. (www.timesofisrael.com/israel-says-it-foiled-hamas-plan-for-coup-against-pa-in-west-bank/)

[62] "Hamas Delegation to Visit Turkey," *Ma'an News Agency* (Palestinian Territories), March 16, 2012; (www.maannews.net/eng/ViewDetails.aspx?ID=468536) & "مشعل ووفد من حركة حماس يلتقي رئيس الوزراء التركي," *Hamas Information Office Website*, October 8, 2013. (www.hamasinfo.net/ar/default.aspx?xyz=U6Qq7k%2bcOd87MD146m9rUxJEpMO%2bi1s7STpp4vS%2fUt0HKm RVD1acVijjinOQOgBfLZoCZz7lptMYVzS3uLdx0MPfjTKdx8fXL7m8XoPzWJ4XAP3ccvAhA2%2fofg5kycQ34K vGJ8XorF%3d)

Speaking at an Istanbul conference of a group headed by Yusef al-Qaradawi, the International Union of Muslim Scholars (IUMS), al-Arouri announced last month that his terrorist group had carried out the kidnapping and killing of three Israeli teens in the West Bank in June. Interestingly, Hamas had denied its responsibility at the time of the attack. But as the war neared its end, with Turkey's deputy prime minister in the audience,[63] al-Arouri took the opportunity to laud the triple murder as a "heroic operation" carried out by Hamas operatives with the broader goal of sparking a new Palestinian uprising.[64]

Al-Arouri is not the only Hamas figure in Turkey, either. In 2011, Israel released 10 Hamas operatives to Turkey as part of the prisoner exchange deal with Hamas that secured the release of Gilad Shalit. Among the Hamas figures believed to have gone to Turkey include Mahmoud Attoun and Taysir Suleiman. Both were sentenced to life terms in Israeli prison for murder. Both men today appear on television and lecture in Turkey and around the world about the merits of Hamas.[65]

Iran

Qatar and Turkey appear to be Hamas's top patrons right now. But Iran still plays a huge role. To be sure, Iran and Hamas have grown apart in recent years, owing primarily to the disagreement over the Syrian civil war. But the relationship is still an enduring one. In a July 2014 letter regarding the latest Gaza conflict, Major General Qassem Suleimani, Commander of Iran's Islamic Revolutionary Guard Corps Qods Force (IRGC-QF), described the leaders of Hamas as "my dear brothers" and reaffirmed Iran's support to the terrorist group.[66]

Iran was one of the early supporters of Hamas. In 1992, Hamas and Iranian officials reached an agreement that led to the formation of a political and military alliance.[67] According to FDD's chairman, testifying in 1995 in his capacity as Director of Central Intelligence, James Woolsey noted that Iran provided more than $100 million to Hamas from 1988 to 1994.[68] In 1993, according to PLO allegations, Iran pledged an annual $30 million subsidy to Hamas.[69] Osama Hamdan, a Hamas representative to Iran in 1994, openly gloated that the growing ties between Hamas and Iran came at the expense of the PLO after the latter's decision to enter into peace

[63] "Başbakan Yardimcisi İşler. Dünya Müslüman Alimler Birliği Toplantisina Katildi," *Milliyet* (Turkey), (http://www.milliyet.com.tr/basbakan-yardimcisi-isler-dunya-musluman-istanbul-verelfotogaleri-4488477/)
[64] "Hamas Admits Kidnapping Israeli Teen," *Associated Press*, August 21, 2014. (www.washingtonpost.com/world/middle_east/hamas-admits-kidnapping-israeli-teens/2014/08/21/6c70b51e-2957-11e4-8b10-7db129976abb_story.html)
[65] Jonathan Schanzer & Michael Argosh, "Lying Down With Dogs," *Foreign Policy*, August 20, 2014. (http://www.foreignpolicy.com/articles/2014/08/20/turkey_hamas_palestine_erdogan_abbas_israel)
[66] Behnam Ben Taleblu, "Analysis: What The Gaza War Means For Iran," *The Long War Journal*, August 1, 2014. (http://www.longwarjournal.org/archives/2014/08/what_the_gaza_war_me.php)
[67] Avraham Sela & Shaul Mishal, *The Palestinian Hamas: Vision, Violence, and Coexistence* (New York: Columbia University Press, 2000), page 97.
[68] R. James Woolsey, "Worldwide Intelligence Review," *Hearing before the Senate Select Committee on Intelligence*, January 10, 1995. (http://archive.org/stream/worldwideintelli00unit/worldwideintelli00unit_djvu.txt)
[69] "Hamas: The Organizations, Goals and Tactics of a Militant Palestinian Organization," *Congressional Research Service*, October 14, 1993. (http://www.fas.org/irp/crs/931014-hamas.htm)

negotiations with Israel.[70] In 1993, Egyptian intelligence reported that Iran was training up to 3,000 Hamas militants.[71] Iran trained Qassam Brigades fighters in both Sudan and Iran. These fighters often returned to the West Bank and Gaza Strip for commando or suicide operations.[72]

Iranian funding continued through the late 1990s,[73] and into the second intifada. But it was not until 2003 and 2004 that the financial relationship deepened. After a series of attacks in the Kingdom of Saudi Arabia by al-Qaeda, the Kingdom elected to reduce its support to violent groups around the region, including Hamas. This left a vacuum that Iran filled. Beginning in 2004, Khaled Meshal began to coordinate more of Hamas's military, political, and financial activities out of Damascus.[74] As he did, Meshal also turned increasingly to Tehran for both financing and training.[75]

Iran became even more vital to Hamas's finances after Hamas's January 2006 electoral victory and the Western embargo that followed. A Hamas spokesman confirmed that Iran "was prepared to cover the entire deficit in the Palestinian budget, and [to do so] continuously." The *Bonyad-e Mostazafan va Janbazan* (Foundation of the Oppressed and War Veterans), a splinter of Iran's IRGC, reportedly opened its coffers to Hamas, providing critical financial support.[76] During a visit by Hamas Prime Minister Ismail Haniyeh to Tehran in December 2006, Iran pledged $250 million in aid to compensate for the Western boycott.[77] Iran is also believed to have assisted in Hamas's overthrow of the Palestinian Authority in the Gaza Strip in 2007.[78]

In October 2007, Secretary of State Condoleeza Rice openly stated her concerns about Iranian support to Hamas during congressional testimony.[79] Rice had plenty of reason to be concerned. A series of Treasury designations in 2006 and 2007 laid bare the extent of Iranian financial support to Hamas. In 2006, Treasury targeted Iran's Bank Saderat, noting that it was "used by the Government of Iran to transfer money to terrorist organizations, including…Hamas."[80] In 2007, the Treasury designated the Iran-based Martyrs Foundation, including its U.S. branch (Goodwill Charitable Organization), and described it as "an Iranian parastatal organization that

---

[70] Zaki Chehab, *Inside Hamas: The Untold Story of the Militant Islamic Movement*. (NY: Nation Books, 2007), pp. 140-142.

[71] Yohanan Ramati, "Islamic Fundamentalism Gaining," *Midstream*. vol. 39, no. 2 (Feb/March 1993), p. 2.

[72] Reuven Paz, "Hamas's Lessons From Lebanon," *Washington Institute for Near East Policy*, May 25, 2000. (http://www.washingtoninstitute.org/policy-analysis/view/hamass-lessons-from-lebanon)

[73] U.S. Department of State, "Patterns of Global Terrorism 1999," April 2000, p. 46. (http://www.state.gov/www/global/terrorism/1999report/patterns.pdf)

[74] For more, see Eben Kaplan, "Profile of Khaled Meshal," *Council on Foreign Relations*, July 13, 2006. (http://www.cfr.org/publication/11111/)

[75] Matthew Levitt, *Hamas: Politics, Charity and Terrorism in the Service of Jihad*, (New Haven CT: Yale University Press, 2006), p.174.

[76] Zaki Chehab, *Inside Hamas: The Untold Story of the Militant Islamic Movement*. (NY: Nation Books, 2007), p. 139.

[77] Meyrav Wurmser, "The Iran-Hamas Alliance," *inFocus Quarterly*, Fall 2007. (http://www.jewishpolicycenter.org/article/57)

[78] Jonathan Halevi, "The Hamas Regime In The Gaza Strip: An Iranian Satellite That Threatens Regional Stability," *Jerusalem Center for Public Affairs*, August 30, 2008. (http://jcpa.org/wp-content/uploads/2012/08/iran_halevi.pdf)

[79] "Rice Says Two-State Solution In The Middle East Is In Jeopardy," *Associated Press*, October 24, 2007. (http://www.haaretz.com/news/rice-says-2-state-solution-in-middle-east-in-jeopardy-1.231838)

[80] U.S. Department of the Treasury, Press Release, "Treasury Cuts Iran's Bank Saderat Off From U.S. Financial System," September 8, 2006. (http://www.treasury.gov/press-center/press-releases/Pages/hp87.aspx)

channels financial support from Iran to several terrorist organizations in the Levant, including ... Hamas."[81] Treasury also designated the IRGC-QF, noting material support to Hamas, among others. Finally, a Treasury Department press release from 2007 claimed that Hamas had substantial assets deposited in Bank Saderat as early as 2005 and that Bank Saderat had transferred several million dollars to Hamas between 2006 and 2007.[82]

In May 2008, *Asharq al-Awsat* reported that Iran was set to provide Hamas with $150 million.[83] The following year, Egypt's then-intelligence chief Omar Suleiman reportedly told the United States that Iran provided Hamas with $25 million per month.[84]

There was also a widespread recognition within the Israeli military that Hamas's fighting capabilities had improved because of Iranian assistance. In March 2008, *The Sunday Times* reported that "Hamas had been sending fighters to Iran for training in both field tactics and weapons technology."[85] Equipped with night vision goggles and other specialized hardware, the professionalism of the new Iranian-trained Hamas military led one veteran intelligence office in Israel to admit, "the Palestinians never looked like this."[86]

Beginning around 2009, Iran also began to increase its efforts to arm Hamas with missiles. The United States received multiple reports of Iranian missile smuggling via Sudan to the Gaza Strip.[87] In March 2011, Israeli authorities boarded the *Victoria* and seized numerous Iranian weapons, including anti-ship missiles, destined for Hamas.[88] During Operation Pillar of Defense in 2012, Hamas fired Iranian-engineered Fajr 5 missiles from Gaza into Israel—an indication that rockets were getting through, despite several successful Israeli interdictions.[89] More recently, in March 2014, the IDF intercepted a Panamanian-flagged cargo vessel identified as the *Klos-C* carrying M-302 rockets and other "advanced weaponry intended for terrorist organizations operating in the Gaza Strip shipped by Iran."[90]

---

[81] U.S. Department of the Treasury, Press Release, "Twin Treasury Actions Take Aim at Hizballah's Support Network," July 24, 2007. (http://www.treasury.gov/press-center/press-releases/Pages/hp503.aspx)

[82] U.S. Department of the Treasury, Press Release, "Fact Sheet: Designation of Iranian Entities and Individuals for Proliferation Activities and Support for Terrorism," October 25, 2007. (http://www.treasury.gov/press-center/press-releases/Pages/hp644.aspx)

[83] "Iran Pledges To Continue Support Of Hamas." *Asharq al-Awsat* (Saudi Arabia), May 26, 2008. (http://www.asharq-e.com/news.asp?section=1&id=12877)

[84] "Admiral Mullen's Meeting With Egis Chief Soliman," *Wikileaks*, April 30, 2009. (http://wikileaks.org/cable/2009/04/09CAIRO746.html)

[85] Marie Colvin, "Iran Arming And Training Hamas Force," *The Sunday Times* (U.K.), March 9, 2008. (Accessed via LexisNexis)

[86] Amos Harel, "Reservists: Hamas Fights Like An Army," *Haaretz* (Israel), November 7, 2007. (http://www.haaretz.com/hasen/spages/921630.html)

[87] "Follow-Up To Information," *Wikileaks*, January 22, 2009: (http://wikileaks.org/cable/2009/01/09STATE5567.html) & "IDF Deputy Chief Of Staff Discusses Gaza Operation Cast Lead And U.S.-Egyptian Roles To Slow Smuggling To Hamas," *Wikileaks*, February 19, 2009. (http://wikileaks.org/cable/2009/02/09TELAVIV422.html)

[88] Yaakov Katz. "Victoria's Secret: The Inside Story Of An Arms-Laden Ship." *The Jerusalem Post* (Israel), March 18, 2011. (http://www.jpost.com/Defense/Article.aspx?id=212683)

[89] Saeed Kamali Dehghan, "Iran Supplied Hamas With Fajr-5 Missile Technology," *The Guardian* (U.K.), November 21, 2012. (http://www.theguardian.com/world/2012/nov/21/iran-supplied-hamas-missile-technology)

[90] David Barnett, "Israeli Navy Intercepts Iranian Weapons Shipment Headed For Gaza," *The Long War Journal*, March 5, 2014. (http://www.longwarjournal.org/archives/2014/03/israeli_navy_interc.php)

During the most recent Gaza conflict, one Iranian official boasted that Tehran is "sending rockets and military aid [to Hamas]."[91] Another official bragged that the estimated 4,000 projectiles launched by Hamas at Israel during the most recent round of fighting "are the blessings of Iran's transfer of technology" to the Palestinian terror group.[92] Hamas also maintains an indigenous rocket-making capability now. The speaker of the Iranian parliament, Ali Larijani, claimed that Hamas gained this capability with the help of Iranian training.[93] And now, after the fighting has stopped, Iran is threatening to arm the West Bank for the next battle with Israel.[94]

It is worth noting here that a key figure in procuring Hamas funds and weapons for Hamas is believed to be a man named Imad al-Alami.[95] As recently as 2013, al-Alami, reportedly met with Larijani.[96] As Hamas's representative to Tehran, al-Alami is a known quantity at the U.S. Treasury, which designated him in 2003.

Treasury, it should be noted, continues to target others involved in the Iran-Hamas financial pipeline. In August 2010, Treasury designated Hushang Allahdad, a senior financial officer of the IRGC-QF who "personally oversees distribution of funds to Levant-based terrorist groups and provides financial support for designated terrorist entities including…Hamas."[97] The following year, the State Department designated Hamas operative Muhammad Hisham Muhammad Isma'il Abu Ghazala, noting his extensive links to Iran.[98] In August 2013, the Treasury designated four members of Hezbollah's leadership including Khalil Harb, who is described as "overseeing work of the Islamic Resistance, including assisting with the smuggling of Hamas…operatives from Syria into the West Bank via Jordan."[99]

Over the last year, however, designations have trailed off somewhat, but not entirely. This may be due, in part, to the Administration's reluctance to sanction Iran during the sensitive Joint Plan

---

[91] Ali Hashem, "Did Iran Train Gaza Rocket Makers?," *Al Monitor*, July 17, 2014. (http://www.al-monitor.com/pulse/originals/2014/07/gaza-rockets-palestine-iran-self-sufficient.html)

[92] Ali Akbar Dareini, "Iran Says Country Has Transferred Missile Technology To Hamas," *Associated Press*, August 4, 2014. (http://www.usnews.com/news/world/articles/2014/08/04/iran-says-it-gave-missile-technology-to-hamas)

[93] "Larijani Says Iran Gave Hamas Its Rocket Know-How," *Naharnet*, July 24. 2014. (http://www.naharnet.com/stories/en/140398)

[94] "Iran 'Will Arm Palestinians' After Israeli Drone Downed," *Agence France Presse*, August 25, 2014, (http://www.dailystar.com.lb/News/Middle-East/2014/Aug-25/268380-iran-will-arm-palestinians-after-israeli-drone-downed-military.ashx#axzz3CYnMfJ8W)

[95] "السيرة الذاتية للأستاذ عماد العلمي," *The Islamic Resistance Movement Information Office Website*, January 30, 2011. (http://www.hamasinfo.net/ar/default.aspx?xyz=U6Qq7k%2bcOd87MD146m9rUxJEpMO%2bi1s7zT6haxRNqZhof%2fFllWqOiUasmwKSW9VlA5e9Ww9qEwuTK3ihIbvwOnDyWpX9PuUIAnsAPtCnfpWbTLB0jhg5kd%2bTUf5C3JuSQeygX3wwXZY%3d)

[96] "Iran Always Ready To Assist Palestinian Fighters: Majlis Speaker," *Press TV* (Iran), January 17, 2013. (http://www.presstv.ir/detail/2013/01/17/284036/iran-always-ready-to-help-palestinians/)

[97] U.S. Department of the Treasury, Press Release, "Fact Sheet: U.S. Treasury Department Targets Iran's Support for Terrorism Treasury Announces New Sanctions Against Iran's Islamic Revolutionary Guard Corps-Qods Force Leadership," August 3, 2010. (http://www.treasury.gov/press-center/press-releases/Pages/tg810.aspx)

[98] U.S. Department of State, Press Release, "Terrorist Designation of HAMAS Operative Muhammad Hisham Muhammad Isma'il Abu Ghazala," September 22, 2011. (http://www.state.gov/r/pa/prs/ps/2011/09/173352.htm)

[99] U.S. Department of the Treasury, Press Release, "Treasury Sanctions Hizballah Leadership," August 22, 2013. (http://www.treasury.gov/press-center/press-releases/Pages/jl2147.aspx)

of Action nuclear negotiations. For participating in these talks, Iran has received billions of dollars in sanctions relief as an inducement to relinquish its illicit nuclear program.

Sudan

Similar to its relationship with Iran, Hamas has long-standing ties with Sudan. The group's members regularly travel to Sudan to attend conferences, as well as to meet with Sudanese officials.[100] According to the State Department's annual *Country Reports on Terrorism*, Hamas fundraises in Sudan and maintains a presence there.[101] Hamas has reportedly established a strong relationship with Sudanese government officials and uses Sudan as a key transit route to facilitate the movement of Iranian weapons to Gaza.[102]

In the 1990s, Hamas maintained offices in Khartoum's Ammarat district,[103] and used Sudanese territory to train its operatives.[104] In 2001, *Maariv* reported that Israeli and U.S. intelligence believed that Sudan had become a "major haven" for terrorists from a number of Middle East terror groups, including Hamas. According to the report, "Iran transfers money to the terrorists in Sudan, provides Iranian trainers, and maintains regular contacts with Hamas and Islamic Jihad men." One security source noted, "many Hamas activists know for a fact that they have a place to run to. Therefore, they go to Sudan, where they can move freely."[105]

In August 2002, Muntasar Talab Salamah Frej, a Palestinian from Gaza, was arrested by the Israel Security Agency (Shin Bet). The indictment against Frej charged him with receiving bomb-making training in Sudan, under the auspices of Hamas, in addition to a number of other terror-related charges.[106] More recently, in February 2010, multiple sources cited a report on the Lebanese *Al-Qanat* website that alleged that Hamas was training operatives in Sudan to fire rockets.[107] In January 2013, a delegation from Hamas's Interior Ministry, led by Fathi Hammad,

[100] "Sudanese President Meets With Hamas Leaders," *Sudan Tribune*, December 29, 2011; (http://www.sudantribune.com/spip.php?article41131) & "News of Terrorism and the Israeli-Palestinian Conflict January 9-15, 2013," *Meir Amit Intelligence and Terrorism Information Center*, January 16, 2013. (http://www.terrorism-info.org.il/Data/articles/Art_20463/E_008_12_626838694.pdf)

[101] U.S. Department of State, "Chapter 3: State Sponsors of Terrorism," August 18, 2011. (http://www.state.gov/j/ct/rls/crt/2010/170260.htm)

[102] Ethan Bronner, "With Longer Reach, Rockets Bolster Hamas Arsenal," *The New York Times*, November 17, 2012. (http://www.nytimes.com/2012/11/18/world/middleeast/arms-with-long-reach-bolster-hamas.html)

[103] Christopher Harmon, "Sudan's Neighbors Accuse It of Training Terrorists," *Christian Science Monitor*, December 19, 1995. (http://www.csmonitor.com/1995/1219/19191.html)

[104] Matthew Levitt, *Hamas: Politics, Charity and Terrorism in the Service of Jihad*, (New Haven: Yale University Press, 2006).

[105] "Israeli, US Intelligence Report Says Sudan Becoming Haven For Hamas, Hezbollah," *BBC Summary of World Broadcasts* (U.K.), March 14, 2001. (Accessed via LexisNexis)

[106] Amos Harel, "Hamas Trains Bomb Experts in Sudan," *Haaretz* (Israel), September 19, 2002. (http://www.haaretz.com/print-edition/news/hamas-trains-bomb-experts-in-sudan-1.33868)

[107] Hillel Fendel, "New Details On Hamas-Iran Ties Revealed," *Arutz Sheva* (Israel), February 21, 2010; (http://www.israelnationalnews.com/News/News.aspx/136111#.UPhdeB2eON4) & "Report: IRGC Training Hamas Operatives In Sudan," *The Middle East Media Research Institute*, accessed January 17, 2013. (http://www.memrijttm.org/content/en/blog_personal.htm?id=2929&param=APT)

visited Khartoum, and reached an agreement that will see Hamas members sent to Sudan for defense training.[108]

Sudan's role as a physical transit point for smuggling operations, particularly to Egypt's Sinai Peninsula, is especially troubling. According to General Carter Ham, formerly of the U.S. Africa Command, "the most grave concern [regarding Iran in Africa] is the transiting of weapons and technology principally, but not exclusively, through Sudan."[109]

In January 2009, Israel tracked a major weapons shipment, which included Fajr missiles, from Iran to Port Sudan. After arriving in Sudan, the weapons were put on a 23-truck convoy that was intended to traverse Egypt's Sinai and end up in the hands of Hamas smugglers near the Gaza border. Israeli sources, who confirmed that "dozens of aircraft" were involved in attacking the convoy, estimated that the shipment was probably the largest ever from Iran to Hamas via Sudan. In addition, *ABC News* reported that a ship carrying weapons off the coast of Sudan was struck by Israel around the same time.[110]

By 2010, Israeli officials learned that Fajr missiles were being "assembled locally after being shipped from Iran to Sudan, trucked across the desert through Egypt, broken down into parts and moved through Sinai tunnels into Gaza." In addition, they discovered that "the smuggling route involves salaried employees from Hamas along the way, and Iranian technical experts traveling on forged passports and government approval in Sudan."[111]

On October 23, 2012, a series of airstrikes took place at the Yarmouk Industrial Complex outside of Khartoum. Sudanese officials quickly blamed Israel,[112] while Israeli officials stayed relatively quiet. Meanwhile, Iran,[113] Hamas,[114] and Hezbollah,[115] condemned the strike and Iran soon sent two naval vessels to Sudan to "convey a message of peace and friendship to the region's

---

[108] "News of Terrorism And The Israeli-Palestinian Conflict January 9-15, 2013," *Meir Amit Intelligence and Terrorism Information Center*, January 16, 2013. (http://www.terrorism-info.org.il/Data/articles/Art_20463/E_008_12_626838694.pdf)

[109] "Leader Of U.S. Africa Command Discusses Security Challenges," *C-SPAN*, December 3, 2012. (http://www.c-span.org/Events/Leader-of-US-Africa-Command-Discusses-Security-Challenges/10737436227/)

[110] Michael James, "Exclusive: Three Israeli Airstrikes Against Sudan," *ABC News*, March 27, 2009. (http://blogs.abcnews.com/politicalradar/2009/03/exclusive-three.html)

[111] Ethan Bronner, "With Longer Reach, Rockets Bolster Hamas Arsenal," *The New York Times*, November 17, 2012. (http://www.nytimes.com/2012/11/18/world/middleeast/arms-with-long-reach-bolster-hamas.html)

[112] "Sudan Blames Israel for Khartoum Arms Factory Blast," *BBC* (U.K.), October 24, 2012. (http://www.bbc.co.uk/news/world-africa-20050781)

[113] "Iran: Israel's Attack On Khartoum Clear Violation Of Int'l Laws," *Fars News Agency* (Iran), October 25, 2012. (http://www.thefreelibrary.com/Iran%3A+Israel's+Attack+on+Khartoum+Clear+Violation+of+int'l+Laws.-a0306326349)

[114] "Hamas Condemns The Treacherous Zionist Aggression On The Brotherly Sudan," *Hamas Information Office Website*, October 25, 2012. (http://www.hamasinfo.net/ar/default.aspx?xyz=U6Qq7k%2BcOd87MDI46m9rUxJEpMO%2Bi1s7uCR8tstCoAho FkEeHxVKGx/Zhaf0o5uUXXuk8WQojeUZ8Cu4KFkzvtBZwfxvdOG%2BLA0LVpZAIGduIJHvY4pPMUpkDt66 65raeozkk27VIyc%3D)

[115] Roi Kais, "Hezbollah Condemns Israeli 'Aggression' Against Sudan," *Ynet News* (Israel), October 25, 2012. (http://www.ynetnews.com/articles/0,7340,L-4297066,00.html)

countries and to provide safety at sea in light of maritime terrorism."[116] It is now believed that the Yarmouk facility was storing Fajr 5 rockets.

Today, Port Sudan is still the preferred hub for the transfer of Iranian weaponry to Hamas in the Gaza Strip. However, because of Egypt's closure of the tunnels, less is getting through, thus rendering Sudan a less important player in the Hamas rocket pipeline. But, to be clear, this was not by choice.

In the meantime, Sudan appears to maintain a number of Hamas charities. For example, the Beirut-based Jerusalem Foundation International (JFI), which was designated in 2012,[117] maintains a presence in Sudan under the name of "Al Quds International Institution."[118] In December 2011, during a visit to Khartoum, Hamas's Ismail Haniyeh participated in a conference organized by the JFI. During his speech, he called for additional financial aid and political support.[119]

As an American Enterprise Institute report notes, Hamas is known to operate "a little business empire" in Sudan.[120] One recent item in the Kuwait-based *Al Seyassah* alleged that Hamas operates a company known as Hassan and Abed International for Roads and Bridges, based in Khartoum.[121] The company appears in at least one Sudanese business listing.[122] The company reportedly also has an unspecified connection to Abdel Baset Hamza, a former acquaintance of a number of al-Qaeda operatives, including Osama bin Laden.[123]

The Gaza Tycoons Club

On a final note, as these two distinguished committees go about tracking Hamas finance, it is worth noting that at least two Hamas figures in Gaza are believed to have significant sums in their personal accounts. This is in addition to the other purported Hamas billionaires—Khaled Meshal and Mousa Abu Marzook—mentioned above.

---

[116] "Iranian Warships Dock In Sudan Port Amid Row With Israel Over Factory Blast," *Al Arabiya* (Saudi Arabia), October 30, 2012. (http://www.alarabiya.net/articles/2012/10/30/246628.html)

[117] U.S. Department of Treasury, Press Release, "Treasury Sanctions Two Hamas-Controlled Charities," October 4. 2012. (http://www.treasury.gov/press-center/press-releases/Pages/tg1725.aspx)

[118] "Contact Address," *Jerusalem Foundation International,* accessed January 15, 2013. (http://www.alquds-online.org/org/index.php?s=6&ss=27)

[119] "The Visits Of Ismail Haniya, Head Of The De-facto Hamas Administration In The Gaza Strip, To Egypt, Sudan, Turkey And Tunisia Were Meant To Strengthen Hamas' Ties With The Various Countries, Reinforce The Legitimacy Of The Hamas Administration And Bolster Haniya's Personal Status," *Meir Amit Intelligence and Terrorism Information Center,* January 17, 2012. (http://www.terrorism-info.org.il/data/pdf/PDF_12_015_2.pdf)

[120] Ronald Sandee. "Islamism, Jihadism And Terrorism In Sudan." *American Enterprise Institute,* August 6, 2004. (http://www.aei.org/files/2004/08/06/20040809_SANDEEremarks.pdf)

[121] "السياسة" تكشف عن قائمة شركات تمول "حماس" بشكل غير شرعي في دول "الخليجي"," *Palestinian Press Office - Denmark,* May 15, 2013. (http://www.fateh.dk/index.php?option=com_content&view=article&id=5703:2012-07-02-15-11-52&catid=122:2012-05-22-08-01-02&Itemid=314)

[122] "Names Of Companies Operating In Sudan," *Sudanese Economic Directory,* accessed May 28, 2013. (http://www.sudabiz.org/directory/com_view.php?pageNum_com=215&totalRows_com=11051&view=all)

[123] Peter Bergen. *Holy War, Inc.: Inside the Secret World of Osama bin Laden,* (New York: Free Press, 2001). p. 124 & Daniel Pearl. "In Sudan Bombing, 'Evidence' Depends On Who Is Viewing It," *The Wall Street Journal,* October 28, 1998. (http://www.danielpearl.org/news_and_press/danielpearl_articles/102898_In_Sudan.pdf)

According to a July 2014 report by the Israeli publication *Globes*, Hamas's Gaza-based Prime Minister Ismail Haniyeh is currently worth approximately $4 billion. Most of his assets are believed to be registered in Gaza under the name of his son-in-law, Nabil, and his 11 other children, as well as in the name of other low-level Hamas officials. All of Haniyeh's 12 children reportedly have houses in the Gaza Strip worth at least $1 million each.[124] It's unclear how much of this property was damaged during the Gaza war.

According to the same report, Ayman Taha, who is responsible for coordination between Hamas's external and internal leadership, has joined the ranks of Hamas's tycoons. He recently constructed a house in the Gaza Strip worth at least $1 million.[125] Taha allegedly purchased properties and made deals for Hamas in the Gaza Strip, ensuring that Hamas officials received their dividends.[126]

Policy Recommendations

There are some steps that Congress and the Administration can take to continue to hinder Hamas finances.

1. Washington should openly encourage Egypt's continued operations against the tunnels, and other operations that have hindered Hamas finances. Egypt, in my estimation, has in some ways done more to weaken Hamas financially than the United States and Israel combined. Cairo has done this because it believes it is in the Egyptian national interest, despite tensions with Washington. Egypt should receive our assistance in this area. Egypt can reportedly benefit from additional technical support in uncovering the tunnels along the Gaza border. There may also be other military equipment that Washington can provide.[127]

2. Qatar should be pressured to cease its funding to Hamas. It should be asked to expel Khaled Meshal and the other figures currently based there. Qatar should also be pressed to freeze all Hamas funds in Qatari banks. If they do not, the U.S. should push forward with new Treasury designations, and not only of Hamas operatives. The designation of Qatari institutions where Hamas parks its cash could send a message to Doha that Washington is serious.

3. Another measure Congress could take is to put a hold on the $11 billion arms deal the U.S. recently signed with Qatar.[128] This deal included: 24 AH-64E Apache attack helicopters,[129] one

---

[124] "הטייקונים של חמאס: ח'אלד משעל שווה 5-2 מיליארד דולר, סגו אבו-מרזוק שווה 3-2 מיליארד דולר," *Globes* (Israel). July 24. 2014. (http://www.globes.co.il/news/article.aspx?did=1000957870)

[125] "הטייקונים של חמאס: ח'אלד משעל שווה 5-2 מיליארד דולר, סגו אבו-מרזוק שווה 3-2 מיליארד דולר," *Globes* (Israel), July 24, 2014; (http://www.globes.co.il/news/article.aspx?did=1000957870) & Doron Peskin, "Hamas Got Rich As Gaza Was Plunged Into Poverty," *YNet News* (Israel), July 15, 2014. (http://www.ynetnews.com/articles/0,7340,L-4543634,00.html)

[126] Doron Peskin, "Hamas Got Rich As Gaza Was Plunged Into Poverty," *YNet News* (Israel), July 15, 2014. (http://www.ynetnews.com/articles/0,7340,L-4543634,00.html)

[127] Interview with Arab diplomat, Washington, DC, September 4, 2014.

[128] U.S. Army Security Assistance Command, Press Release, "U.S., Qatar Sign Letters on $11 Billion in Helicopters, Defense Systems," July 18, 2014. (http://www.army.mil/article/130183/U_S__Qatar_Sign_Letters_on__11_Billion_in_Helicopters__Defense_Syste ms/)

MIM-104F Patriot PAC-3 missile defense system,[130] and 500 Javelin guided missiles.[131] There is also a Boeing deal in the works for three 737 Airborne Early Warning and Control (AEW&C) aircraft,[132] not to mention other possible sales.[133] Such deals should be put on hold until Qatar's financing of Hamas is addressed.

4. Yet another Congressional measure that could pressure Qatar is to order an assessment of the cost and effort needed to remove U.S. personnel from the al-Udaid airbase. There are other countries in the region willing to host our military. We should at least see what would be needed to make the transition. This could let the Qataris know how serious we are about their role in financing Hamas, not to mention their support of a host of other violent non-state actors throughout the Middle East.

5. Similarly, Turkey should be pressured to cease its funding to Hamas. It should be asked to expel Saleh al-Arouri and the other figures currently based there. Ankara should also be pressed to freeze all Hamas funds in Turkish banks. If they do not, the U.S. should push forward with new Treasury designations. This should include Hamas operatives, front companies, charities, and Turkish banks that contain Hamas accounts. It might also include the IHH, the flotilla charity that is close to the ruling AK Party and has long been suspected of supporting Hamas.

6. Security and intelligence cooperation is reportedly quite good between Ankara and Washington. Congress and the Administration may be able to work through these various agencies, using both carrots and sticks, to exert pressure on Turkey to halt its cooperation with Hamas.

7. Washington may also have some leverage with Turkey through pending arms sales. Ankara is currently set to receive two 737 Peace Eagle Airborne Early Warning and Control (AEW&C) aircraft from the United States. In February, Turkey signed a deal with U.S. helicopter manufacture Sikorsky to co-produce 109 S-90 Black Hawk Helicopters.[134] In August, the State

---

[129] U.S. Defense Security Cooperation Agency, Press Release, "Qatar – AH-64D Apache Block III Longbow Attack Helicopters," July 12, 2014. (http://www.dsca.mil/major-arms-sales/qatar-ah-64d-apache-block-iii-longbow-attack-helicopters).

[130] Tom Kington, "Raytheon Aims To Sign $2B Qatar Patriot Deal By Year End," *Defense News*, July 15, 2014. (http://www.defensenews.com/article/20140715/SHOWSCOUT15/307150022/Raytheon-Aims-Sign-2B-Qatar-Patriot-Deal-by-Year-End).

[131] U.S. Defense Security Cooperation Agency, Press Release, "Qatar – Javelin Missiles," March 28, 2013. (http://www.dsca.mil/major-arms-sales/qatar-javelin-missiles).

[132] Gareth Jennings, "Qatar To Procure 737 AEW&C," *IHS Jane's*, March 27, 2014. (http://www.janes.com/article/36118/qatar-to-procure-737-aew-c)

[133] U.S. Defense Security Cooperation Agency, Press Release, "Qatar – AN/FPS-132 Block 5 Early Warning Radar," July 29, 2013; (http://www.dsca.mil/major-arms-sales/qatar-anfps-132-block-5-early-warning-radar) U. S. Defense Security Cooperation Agency, Press Release, "Qatar – Terminal High Altitude Area Defense (THAAD)," November 5, 2012; (http://www.dsca.mil/major-arms-sales/qatar-terminal-high-altitude-area-defense-thaad) & Salman Siddiqui, "Rafale can 'Easily Meet Qatar's Defence Needs'," *Gulf Times*, March 31, 2014. (http://www.gulf-times.com/qatar/178/details/386596/rafale-can-%E2%80%98easily-meet-qatar%E2%80%99s-defence-needs%E2%80%99)

[134] Burak Bekdil, "Turkey, Sikorsky Sign $3.5 Billion Helicopter Deal," *Defense News*, February 21, 2014. (http://www.defensenews.com/article/20140221/DEFREG01/302210022/Turkey-Sikorsky-Sign-3-5-Billion-Helicopter-Deal)

Department approved a $320 million sale of AIM-120C-7 AMRAAM missiles to Turkey.[135] Earlier this year, the State Department approved a $170 million sale of up to 48 MK 48 Mod 6 torpedoes to Turkey.[136] Turkey also signed a deal for the purchase of six CH-47F Chinook heavy-lift helicopters for $400 million.[137] There are a great many other deals in the works.[138] They, too, can be put on hold if Turkey does not cooperate.

8. Regardless of what steps are taken, Congress should call for GAO investigations and intelligence assessments of both countries. Dedicated hearings on each country may also be useful. Both Turkey and Qatar serve as U.S. allies while simultaneously qualifying as state sponsors of terrorism, to the letter of U.S. law. And the problems do not end with Hamas. Both countries have been involved in a plethora of illicit financial activity with a wide array of terrorist groups and rogue states. To be clear, the goal is to change the behavior of both countries and to preserve these alliances, if at all possible.

9. While Washington has no pending arms sales to Iran, it may have some leverage with Iran through the nuclear negotiating process. Washington should consider demanding a cessation of Hamas finance as part of a final package in the ongoing JPOA negotiations. Indeed, Iran's support to a wide array of terrorist groups has received scant discussion during the 10 months of the talks. If the talks are extended yet again, there should be no further sanctions relief granted until Iran has verifiably halted its terrorism support, along with other important concessions directly tied to the nuclear challenge. This is, to put it mildly, a sensitive issue, given how much is at stake with the JPOA talks. But it may be the only leverage America has with regard to Iran's support for terrorism, outside of traditional sanctions.

[135] U.S. Defense Security Cooperation Agency, Press Release, "Turkey – AIM-120C-7 AMRAAM Missiles," August 12, 2014. (http://www.dsca.mil/major-arms-sales/turkey-aim-120c-7-amraam-missiles)
[136] U.S. Defense Security Cooperation Agency, Press Release, "Republic of Turkey – MK 48 Torpedoes," May 12, 2014. (http://www.dsca.mil/major-arms-sales/republic-turkey-mk-48-torpedoes)
[137] Umit Enginsoy & Burak Bekdil, "Turkey Signs Deal To Buy Six CH-47 Copters." *Defense News*, August 15, 2011. (http://www.defensenews.com/article/20110815/DEFSECT01/108150302/Turkey-Signs-Deal-Buy-Six-CH-47-Copters)
[138] U.S. Department of Defense, Press Release, "Contracts," August 20, 2014;
(http://www.defense.gov/contracts/contract.aspx?contractid=5356&source=GovDelivery) U.S. Department of Defense, Press Release, "Contracts," August 28, 2014;
(http://www.defense.gov/contracts/contract.aspx?contractid=5363&source=GovDelivery) U.S. Department of Defense, Press Release, "Contracts." August 6, 2014;
(http://www.defense.gov/contracts/contract.aspx?contractid=5345&source=GovDelivery) U.S. Department of Defense, Press Release, "Contracts." August 5, 2014;
(http://www.defense.gov/contracts/contract.aspx?contractid=5344&source=GovDelivery) U.S. Department of Defense, Press Release, "Contracts," July 31, 2014;
(http://www.defense.gov/contracts/contract.aspx?contractid=5341&source=GovDelivery) Raytheon, Press Release. "Raytheon to Provide Torpedo Integration on Alenia Aermacchi Aircraft for Turkish Navy," July 17, 2014;
(http://www.marketwatch.com/story/raytheon-to-provide-torpedo-integration-on-alenia-aermacchi-aircraft-for-turkish-navy-2014-07-17) U.S. Department of Defense, Press Release. "Contracts," June 25, 2014;
(http://www.defense.gov/contracts/contract.aspx?contractid=5315&source=GovDelivery) U.S. Department of Defense, Press Release, "Contracts," April 7, 2014;
(http://www.defense.gov/Contracts/Contract.aspx?ContractID=5257) U.S. Department of Defense, Press Release, "Contracts." December 17, 2013; (http://militaryedge.org/articles/boeing-awarded-contract-harpoon-missiles/) & U.S. Department of Defense, Press Release, "Contracts," December 4, 2013.
(http://www.defense.gov/contracts/contract.aspx?contractid=5178)

10. Regardless of what the nuclear talks yield, Iran's terrorism finance activities must continue to be punished through sanctions. There appears to be a temptation on the part of the P5+1 to welcome Iran back into the formal financial sector if a deal is reached. This is exactly what Hamas and other terror groups are waiting for. Washington must remain committed to disrupting the Iran-Hamas pipeline, and designate more Iranian entities that finance Hamas. Treasury must continue to enforce the existing sanctions, as well.

11. With regard to Sudan, America lacks leverage after years of sanctions and punitive measures. But two areas of focus could yield some results: the border with Egypt and Port Sudan. If both are monitored more carefully by U.S. intelligence and other allied services, it may be possible to prevent new Iranian weapons and material from reaching the Gaza Strip.

On behalf of the Foundation for Defense of Democracies, I thank you again for inviting me to testify before these distinguished subcommittees.

Ms. ROS-LEHTINEN. Thank you very much.

Mr. Jorisch.

STATEMENT OF MR. AVI JORISCH, SENIOR FELLOW FOR COUNTERTERRORISM, AMERICAN FOREIGN POLICY COUNCIL

Mr. JORISCH. Good morning, Chairman, Ranking Members, distinguished members of the subcommittees. I am honored to appear before these distinguished committees to address a subject of great importance to our country and the world. I am also pleased to sit alongside my accomplished colleagues, Jonathan Schanzer and Steven Cook.

One of the most effective ways of countering radical Islamic organizations such as Hamas is to have an exhaustive understanding of their financing in order to cut off their economic lifeblood. It is in the highest interests of the United States to force radical organizations to pay a political and economic price for their barbaric policies and ultimately shut them down.

Hamas' budget is between $500 million and $1 billion annually. In the last 7 years, Hamas has passed four budgets. In its most recent budget, 27 percent was to come from domestic revenue. The remaining 73 was to be covered by foreign donations. It is estimated that Hamas collected about $175 million annually from the tunnels, which served as the main source of their domestic revenue collection.

International aid to Hamas has historically come from U.S.-designated state sponsors of terror, including Iran, Syria, and Sudan. But more recently, Qatar and Turkey have stepped up their giving. From 2006 through 2011, Iran served as Hamas' largest donor, contributing some $250 million to $300 million annually. Historically, Hamas has provided—I beg your pardon, Iran has provided Hamas with weapons, technical assistance, and military training. But in 2011 there was a near total rupture in the relationship when Hamas refused to support the Assad regime in Syria.

Israel's operation Protective Edge has brought Hamas and Iran closer, and we are now witnessing a reestablishment of bilateral relations. From 1999 through 2011, Hamas used Damascus as their primary political base of operations. But in 2012, the group announced its support for the Syrian opposition. As a Sunni organization, Hamas decided to support its fellow Sunni jihadis. Naturally, the Assad regime cut off Hamas.

For Qatar, when Hamas lost funding in and support from Syria and Iran, it turned to the other Sunni regional powers, principally Qatar and Turkey. While it is difficult to say precisely how much financial support Qatar provides to Hamas, in 2012, the Emir pledged more than $400 million. Turkey provides strong political support and is also rumored to donate up to $300 million annually to Hamas.

Ideologically, Turkey, above and beyond Hamas' other donors, has supported the Hamas world view and their barbaric agenda. Ankara also provides comfort and support to some of the organization's most important leaders. For its part, Sudan has served as a willing waystation for years for any weapons shipped to Gaza. As Dr. Schanzer pointed out, in four instances over the last 5 years,

Israel is reported to have bombed arms shipments and Sudanese weapons factories.

U.S. policy regarding terrorist organizations and their rogue financial supporters has unfortunately been inconsistent, to say the very least. On the one hand, President Obama has waged war against ISIS; on the other hand, he has proven himself open to working with Hamas and concomitantly negotiating with Iran, which may well be the biggest threat of all to Western liberal democracies.

Hamas' strategy and ideology are almost identical to Sunni groups such as ISIS and al-Qaeda, and Shiite organizations, like Hezbollah and the Clerical Elite, that governs Iran today. Hamas fires rockets from heavily populated areas into Israel's major cities. It sends its members on suicide bombing missions. ISIS kidnaps and beheads journalists, and Iran is marching toward a nuclear bomb while using terror as an operational weapon.

Madam Chairman, I have three primarily policy recommendations for the subcommittees to consider.

First, the U.S. should cease all disbursement of aid to the Palestinian Authority as a result of the unity government formed between Hamas and Fatah this past June. Reversing years of U.S. foreign policy of not engaging in any way, shape, or form with a designated terrorist entity, Secretary of State John Kerry declared the U.S. would cooperate with the technocratic government.

Two, in light of Qatar and Turkey's relationship with Hamas, the United States should threaten to blacklist both countries, both for being state sponsors of terror or for disrupting the Middle East peace process. Congress should make clear that any form of financial or material support for terrorist groups such as Hamas violates U.S. counterterrorism laws.

And finally, three, the United States should declare unequivocally that Hamas and al-Qaeda, including its affiliates such as ISIS, are ideologically one and the same and employ similar tactics. The West defeated each of the 20th century's hostile ideologies using the full panoply of military, economic, diplomatic, and ideological weapons. Today's greatest challenge—radical Islam—deserves no less attention and a multi-partite attack on so dangerous a threat to the life and principles that we and our allies hold dear.

Thank you, ma'am.

[The prepared statement of Mr. Jorisch follows:]

Hamas' Benefactors: A Network of Terror

Testimony before the
U.S. House of Representatives
Committee on Foreign Affairs
Subcommittee on the Middle East and North Africa
&
Subcommittee on Terrorism, Non-Proliferation and Trade

9 September 2014

Avi Jorisch
Senior Fellow
American Foreign Policy Council

Good morning, Ms. Chairman and Members of the House Committee on Foreign Affairs. My name is Avi Jorisch and I serve as a Senior Fellow for Counterterrorism at the American Foreign Policy Council. I have previously served at the Treasury Department's office of Terrorism and Financial Intelligence, as a liaison to the Department of Homeland Security and as a consultant for the Department of Defense. I am honored to appear before this distinguished Committee to address a subject of great importance to our country and the world.

One of the most effective ways of countering radical Islamic organizations such as Hamas is to have an exhaustive understanding of their sources of funding in order to cut off the economic lifeblood that enable terrorist operations to function. Today, the Hamas budget is between $500 million and 1 billion annually. These funds derive principally from state sponsors such as Iran; "frenemy" states such as Qatar and Turkey; and from the heavy taxation of Hamas constituents in Gaza. To a lesser extent, the funds come from radical organizations such as Hizballah; Arab and Islamic institutions that also carry out relief and developmental projects; and private donations through various non-governmental organizations.

It is in the highest interests of the United States, as a liberal democracy, to force radical organizations to pay a political and economic price for their barbaric policies and governance, and ultimately, to close them down entirely for all time. Unfortunately, in recent years, political considerations have progressively displaced or rolled back the serious progress that had been made on draining the financial swamp in which terrorists and terror-supporting regimes operate.

As the recent hostilities in Gaza demonstrate, Hamas is a rogue regime that deliberately seeks civilian casualties on both sides as the major thrust of its military strategy. The battle being fought by Israel is part of a long-term war that other liberal societies will ultimately have to fight. Sooner or later, most democracies will face the same challenge with which Israel is struggling today: how to defend themselves from ruthless enemies who deliberately place civilians in harm's way, while also retaining the basic values upon which open societies are based. It is unlikely that the United States will avoid this challenge at home: terrorists are carefully monitoring how the world responds to the tactics employed by organizations such as Hamas in Gaza and ISIS in Iraq and Syria as part of their future planning.

The challenge, of course, is to make this new kind of war -- with its deliberate effort to ensure civilian casualties on both sides -- unacceptable, while protecting the values that democracies cherish. Certainly, U.S. lawmakers and policymakers have the highest responsibility to learn all they can from Israel's experience with terrorist organizations that seize power.

Brief Background

Hamas, an acronym for "Islamic Resistance Movement," is a militant Palestinian Sunni Islamist organization that has governed the Gaza Strip since 2007. Created in 1987, it is the Palestinian wing of the Muslim Brotherhood, and gained notoriety for multiple suicide bombings and other attacks directed against civilians – including American citizens – as well as against Israeli military and security forces. Hamas, however, has also established an extensive network of social services, hospitals, education systems, and libraries for the Arab residents of the West Bank and Gaza.

A major cause of the latest round of fighting between Israel and Hamas was the organization's economic woes and declining revenue. Traditionally, Hamas has had three sources of funding: taxation of residents of Gaza; taxation of goods entering or leaving Gaza Strip through Israel or Egypt; and financial largesse from "sugar daddy" regimes. All three sources have come under heavy fire in recent years.

Israel imposed a blockade on the Gaza Strip beginning in 2007, following Hamas' rise to power there. The blockade included most exports and imports, which hampered domestic business activity and reduced the taxes Hamas collected. Moreover, since 2007 the Gazan economy has relied on Israel's permitting a limited quantity of goods to enter and leave the Strip—legal commerce that has been supplemented by a robust smuggling business through Egypt.

When the regime of Egypt's Muslim Brotherhood under Mohammed Mursi fell in 2013, Hamas lost a second vital source of income. During his time in office, Mursi allowed goods and materiel freely to enter Gaza, which enabled Hamas to secure cash and hard goods, in addition to taxing anything that went over land or underground in tunnels. By contrast, the current Egyptian regime, headed by General Abdel Fatah el-Sisi, has shown a strong desire to remove Hamas from power. To that end, the Sisi government ordered the destruction of all tunnels and cut off Hamas economically and politically.[1] Losing this source of income was a catastrophic fiscal blow to Hamas.

Additionally, Iran has traditionally served as one of Hamas' largest donors. In 2011, however, when Hamas began supporting Sunni jihadis fighting the Syrian regime, both the Islamic Republic and the Assad regime cut off aid. To fill that void, Hamas began relying on Qatar and Turkey.

It is revealing that, even as Hamas was negotiating the latest cease-fire with Israel, its chief demands included economic concessions such as lifting the Israeli blockade, opening border crossings to Egypt and Israel, and building an airport and seaport. Hamas sees economics as the primary means to consolidate power, while Israel views the group's demands as an attempt to continue importing weapons and thus to perpetuate a long war of attrition.

With the end of hostilities, Hamas has extracted from the cease-fire much-needed political and economic gains that will allow it to revive itself. For example, under the terms of the deal, Israel agreed to open border crossings and allow humanitarian assistance and building material to enter Gaza. Additionally, the fishing zone off the coast of Gaza has now been extended to six miles. For its part, Egypt agreed to open

---

[1] "Egypt court orders tunnels to Gaza destroyed." al-Jazeera, February 26, 2013. Available online (www.aljazeera.com/news/middleeast/2013/02/201322619219970812.html).

the Rafah crossing between Gaza and Sinai. Sami Abu Zuhri, a Hamas spokesperson gloatingly declared, "We announce the victory today after achieving our goals."[2]

Budgets from 2009-Present

Any analysis of Hamas' finances must focus on the organization's budget. When it seized control of the Gaza Strip in 2007, Hamas took responsibility for some million and a half Palestinians. With each passing year, it has submitted an ever-larger budget to its legislative council. Not surprisingly, these budgets have lacked transparency, accuracy, or professionalism

Before 2007, Hamas' budget was estimated at about $4-5 billion per month. Its first budget following its 2006 electoral victory was submitted in 2009 and valued at $428 million. In 2010, it grew to $540 million; in 2011, to $630 million; and in 2012, it reached $769 million. Its 2013 budget, the last submitted, was for $897 million

The last budget submitted projected $243 million in domestic revenue, or 27% of the total. The estimated deficit of $654 million, equaling 73% of the total, was to be covered by foreign donations. Each budget principally consists of four items: wages, operating expenses, social welfare programs and development projects.[3]

Going through the motions of passing a budget are part of an attempt by the organization to secure international recognition and prove that it is managing the Strip in a professional manner.[4]

---

[2] "Gaza ceasefire: what Israel and Hamas gained and lost," The Week, August 27, 2014. Available online (www.theweek.co.uk/world-news/gaza/60121/gaza-ceasefire-what-israel-and-hamas-gained-and-lost).
[3] An exact budget breakdown for 2013 consisted of: 1)**Wages:** $449 million, equaling 50%, covering salaries of 42,000 employees in the Hamas government's bureaucratic apparatus; 2) **Operating expenses:** $103 million, equaling 11.48%, covering government ministry expenses, water and electricity services, travel missions, and mailing expenses; 3) **Social welfare/pensions:** $110 million, equaling 12.26%, covering expenses for various entitlement programs. 4) **Capital and development:** $235 million, equaling 26%, covering new assets and development projects for roads, schools, etc. For comprehensive budget numbers, see "Hamas Budget a Small Step Toward Transparency," AlMonitor, Januar 21, 2013. Available online (www.al-monitor.com/pulse/iw/originals/2013/01/hamas-budget-transparency.html).
[4] Throughout the last four years, Hamas has been widely off the mark in its projected budget figures both for expenses accrued and actual revenue spent. For example, in 2012, projected revenue was $173 million, whereas actual revenues were $221 million. In 2013, projected expenditures were estimated at $869 million, but actual spending did not exceed $445 million. According to Omar Shaban, founder and director of PalThink for Strategic Studies, a Gaza-based "think-and-do-tank," these numbers reflect either a lack of professional experience in setting budgets or a deliberate effort to overestimate expenses in order to secure additional financial support from the international community. "Hamas Budget a Small Step Toward Transparency," AlMonitor, Januar 21, 2013. Available online (www.al-monitor.com/pulse/iw/originals/2013/01/hamas-budget-transparency.html).

Domestic Revenue

The draconian Hamas tax regime provides a window into how the organization has been able to maintain power and provide its constituents with basic government services, while funding the construction of smuggling tunnels through which goods and weapons were transferred.

It is estimated that Hamas has collected about $175 million in annual tax revenues from the tunnels,[5] which are a main source of domestic revenue collection. Prior to 2007, tunnels were built to smuggle weapons to the Palestinians. Since the imposition of the Israeli blockade, they have also been used to import food, medicine, cigarettes, building materials, cash-filled bags, and drugs. Some of the tunnels were crudely built; others were sophisticated and included rail tracks and fuel pipes.

Some of the most lucrative – and heavily taxed - items coming through the tunnels appear to have been fuel, gravel, cement, and steel.[6]

- **Fuel:** In Egypt, a liter of gasoline costs approximately 1.6 NIS (New Israeli Shekels, the currency used in Gaza), while in Israel, a liter costs 7.5 NIS. Hamas would reportedly buy its gasoline in Egypt, smuggle it into Gaza, and charge 3 NIS per liter in taxes alone. At roughly 4.5 NIS a litter, Gazans considered it to be a bargain.

- **Building Material:** According to *TheMarker*, an open-source financial newspaper in Israel, smugglers paid Hamas 20 NIS ($5.83) for each ton of cement, 10 NIS for every ton of gravel, and 50 NIS for every ton of steel. These materials alone reportedly netted Hamas up to 4.2 million NIS per month ($1.2 million).[7]

State Sponsorship

International donations to Hamas and arms for the organization have historically come from U.S.-designated state sponsors of terror, including Iran, Syria, and Sudan. But more recently, "frenemy" states such as Qatar and Turkey have stepped up their

---

[5] "Behind Hamas' guns, a serious problem of dough," Haaretz, August 1, 2014. Available online (www.haaretz.com/news/diplomacy-defense/.premium-1.608344).
[6] Ibid.
[7] Ibid.

giving, thus providing an important lifeline in aiding and abetting Hamas' ability to engage in terror.

Iran/Hizballah

The Iranian government, a U.S-designated sponsor of terrorism, has for years used state-owned banks, an array of front companies, and other deceptive techniques to evade the controls of responsible financial institutions and support radical Islamist organizations such as Hamas, Palestinian Jihad, and Hizballah. From 2006-2011, Iran served as Hamas' single largest foreign donor, contributing some $250-$300 million annually. [8]

Historically, Iran has served as Hizballah's primary enabler of terrorism. In addition to money, Iran has provided weapons, technical assistance, and military training to Hamas. This all-inclusive package of support strengthened the organization's military capabilities as well as enriched its government bureaucracy.

In 2011, there was a near-total rupture in the relationship, caused by Hamas' refusal to support the Assad regime in Syria, an adherent of the Islamic Republic's radical policy. Moreover, Assad's Alawi sect is a loosely affiliated offshoot of Shia Islam, the dominant strain of Islamic belief in Iran. Hamas, a Sunni organization, actively supported the Sunni jihadis fighting Assad.

As a result of this rift, Hamas removed its permanent representative from its embassy in Tehran, and Iran stopped the flow of funds to Hamas and significantly reduced the flow of arms.

Traditionally, Iran has viewed Palestinian extremist organizations as an integral part of its "axis of resistance" against Israel. Both the Islamic Republic and Hizballah in Lebanon have supported Hamas and Palestinian Islamic Jihad to gain a foothold in the Gaza strip and thereby establish a strong base of support there.

Israel's Operation Protective Edge, which began in earnest in early July 2014, has brought Hamas and Iran closer and we are now witnessing a significant re-establishment of bilateral relations. Iran's Supreme Leader, Ali Khamenei, has once

---

[8] "Iran cuts Hamas funding over Syria," The Telegraph. May 31, 2013. Available online (www.telegraph.co.uk/news/worldnews/middleeast/palestinianauthority/10091629/Iran-cuts-Hamas-funding-over-Syria.html).

again called for arming the West Bank and Gaza, which senior Iranian officials and policy analysts on both sides of the Atlantic interpret as an operative directive to resume military aid to Hamas.

Iran's support for radical organizations is a direct continuation of its policy to use terror as a tool against Israel and the West. In the months ahead, it is all but certain that the Islamic Revolutionary Guard Corps (IRGC) and specifically, its Qods Force, will increase contact with and support of Hamas and Palestinian Islamic Jihad.

Syria

Since Hamas' founding in 1987 and particularly since the late 1990s, the group has received extensive moral, political, material, and to a small degree, financial support from Syria. Additionally, its top military brigade leadership received extensive military training there. Syria served as critical base for Hamas, without which the organization could not have operated effectively for many years.

Beginning in 1999, the group's leadership began using Damascus as its primary base of operations. Until the outbreak of the Syrian civil war in 2011, the organization's highest decision-making body, the Political Bureau, operated in Syria. Additionally, Khalid Mashaal, the political leader of Hamas, lived and operated in Damascus until he fled to Qatar in 2012.

After the outbreak of the civil war in 2011, Hamas members began leaving Syria and distancing themselves from the Assad regime. In 2012, group officials announced its support for the Syrian opposition,[9] which prompted the Syrian government to kill some Hamas leaders still in the country and to close all local Hamas offices.[10] Finally, in 2013, Hamas was reported to be training the opposition Free Syrian Army.[11]

Qatar

For years, Qatar has been attempting to raise its profile as a major regional player. Fundamentally, Qatar is interested in power. To that end, it will do business with

---

[9] "Hamas ditches Assad, backs Syrian revolt," Reuters, February 24, 2012. Available online (www.reuters.com/article/2012/02/24/us-syria-palestinians-idUSTRE81N1CC20120224).

[10] "Syria Shuts Down Hamas Offices," Arutz Sheva, November 6, 2012. Available online (www.israelnationalnews.com/News/News.aspx/161750#.USZRsjfN8fS).

[11] "Military wing of Hamas training Syrian rebels," May 4, 2013. Available online (www.jpost.com/Middle-East/Hamas-reportedly-training-Syrian-rebels-in-Damascus-308795).

anyone that serves their interest, be it al-Qaeda, Hamas, Israel or the United States. They have also maintained a major rivalry with Saudi Arabia and have a propensity to engage in anything that will overshadow their giant neighbor. In line with Qatar's regional aspirations, it serves as an operational headquarters for Hamas and is home to the group's most important leader, Khalid Mashaal.

When Hamas lost the funding and support of Syria and Iran, it turned to other Sunni regional powers, principally Qatar and Turkey. Egypt, Saudi Arabia, Israel, and other Middle Eastern states have accused the two of undermining regional security by supporting this radical organization. While it is difficult to say precisely how much financial support Qatar provides to Hamas, in October 2012, Sheikh Hamad bin Khalifa al-Thani, Qatar's emir at the time, pledged more than $400 million.

Politically, Qatar has been indispensible to Hamas. In addition to serving as the group's chief negotiator with Israel, Egypt, Saudi Arabia, and the United States in the recent Gaza hostilities, Doha has played a key role in strengthening the relationship between Hamas and various European countries. It has also acted as a mediator between Hamas and Jordan, arranging a meeting in January 2012 between Khalid Mashaal – who was banished from Jordan in 1999 - and Jordan's King Abdullah II.[12]

Turkey

Turkey serves as Hamas' other strong Sunni regional ally, second only to Qatar. It provides political support and is rumored to donate up to $300 million annually to Hamas.[13] Turkish President Recep Tayyip Erdogan has been a staunch supporter of Hamas, propping up the organization throughout the international arena. Ideologically speaking, Turkey, above and beyond Hamas' other donors, has supported the Hamas world-view and their barbaric agenda.

Ankara also provides comfort and support to some of the organization's most important leaders. For example, Saleh al-Arouri, a founder of the Hamas military wing, the Izz al-Dinal Qassam Brigades, both reside in Turkey. According to Israeli

---

[12]"Jordan's king receives Hamas leader," al-Jazeera, January 30, 2012. Available online (www.aljazeera.com/news/middleeast/2012/01/2012129133314758190.html).
[13] "Turkey To Grant Hamas $300 Million," International Middle East Media Center, December 3, 2011. Available online (www.imemc.org/article/62607). See also "Turkey may provide Hamas with $300 million in annual aid." Haaretz, January 28, 2012. Available online (www.haaretz.com/news/diplomacy-defense/turkey-may-provide-hamas-with-300-million-in-annual-aid-1.409708).

intelligence, Hamas' Turkish office is responsible for directing, funding, and providing the organizational infrastructure for terror activity in the West Bank. The Turkish office also serves as a hub for converting European students who are members of Muslim Brotherhood associations into members of Hamas.[14]

Sudan

For years, Sudan has served as a willing way station for Iranian weapons shipped from the Islamic Republic to Hamas in Gaza. In four instances over the last five years, Israel has reportedly bombed these arms shipments and Sudanese weapons factories. In 2009, Israel struck a truck convoy with arms destined for Hamas, and in 2012, it hit an arms factory. This past March, Israel intercepted the Klos-C, a ship carrying arms for Hamas, just off Port Sudan. And in June, Israel bombed a Sudanese long-range arsenal storing missiles intended for Hamas.

Conclusions

There must be no accommodation with radical Islamic terrorist organizations. U.S. policy regarding terrorist organizations and their rogue financial supporters with Islamist agendas has, unfortunately, been inconsistent. On the one hand, President Obama has waged war against ISIS. On the other hand, he has proven himself open to working with Hamas and concomitantly negotiating with the Islamic Republic of Iran, which may well be the biggest threat of all to Israel and the West.

Hamas' strategy and ideology are almost identical to those of the Sunni ISIS and al-Qaeda, as well as of radical Shiite organizations, including Hizballah, the IRGC, and the clerical elite that governs Iran today. Each of these groups is attempting to force Western liberal democracies into a lose-lose situation by rejecting the basic norms of warfare, which are intended to protect civilian populations. Hamas fires rockets from heavily populated areas in Gaza into Israel's major cities and sends its members to engage in suicide bombing, while groups such as ISIS kidnap and behead journalists. Iran is marching towards a nuclear bomb while using terror as an operational weapon.

It appears that Israel and the region as a whole are destined to face this deadly challenge for the foreseeable future. And despite the complacency and even hostility to Israel in some democracies, sooner or later, even those far from the Middle East

---

[14] "Hamas Current Trends 2012-2013," Israeli Security Agency (n.d.).

will confront the very danger Israel has faced this summer. Hamas, Hizballah, their patron Iran, al Qaeda, and other jihadi groups are sworn enemies of the West and of all liberal democracies. They are constantly seeking ways to undermine the strength of the free world. Forms of aggression first used against Israel have inevitably been turned against other countries: airline hijackings, suicide terrorism, and now, the use of civilians as human shields.

Ultimately, liberal democracies must realize that it is in their own interest to make it at once more difficult and more expensive for illicit actors to operate. It is time to recognize the threat posed by radical Islam and take the necessary steps to pursue those who have the motive, the opportunity and the capacity to harm us all.

Policy Recommendations

1. *The US should cease all disbursement of aid the Palestinian Authority as a result of the unity government formed between Hamas and Fatah.* This past June, after seven years of bitter fighting, Fatah and Hamas formed a historic unity government. Reversing years of U.S. foreign policy of not engaging in any way with a designated terrorist entity, Secretary of State John Kerry declared that the U.S. would cooperate with the technocrat government. Secretary Kerry vowed that the U.S would closely monitor its compliance with the Quartet's principles of non-violence, recognition of Israel, and acceptance of the previous agreements. As the recent Gaza hostilities demonstrate beyond a shadow of doubt, Hamas has no intension of adhering to a single one of the three aforementioned principles.

2. *In light of Qatar and Turkey's relationship with Hamas, the United States should threaten to blacklist the two, both for being state sponsors of terror and for disrupting the Middle East peace process.* Turkey's NATO membership and the Al Udeid US military base in Qatar have been cited as pretexts to do little to stop these countries' support of Hamas. Congress should make clear that any form of financial or material support for terrorist groups such as Hamas violates U.S. counterterrorism laws. In fact, Executive Order 12947, issued on January 23, 1995, specifically prohibits Americans from engaging in transactions with Hamas, naming it as one of several terrorist groups that "threaten to disrupt the Middle East peace process."

3. *The United States should declare unequivocally that Hamas and al-Qaeda, including its affiliates such as ISIS, are ideologically one and the same and employ similar tactics.* Today's wealthiest Islamic republics — Saudi Arabia, Iran and Sudan — and their consistent funding

of terror demonstrates the reason we must take the ever greater problem of radical Islam seriously. These three regimes account for the vast majority of funding, ideological support and protection for terrorist organizations and jihadis around the globe. The West defeated each of the 20th century's hostile ideologies using the full panoply of military, economic, diplomatic and ideological weapons. Today's greatest challenge—radical Islam—deserves no less serious a multi-partite attack on so dangerous a threat to the life and principles that we and our allies hold dear.

Ms. Ros-Lehtinen. Thank you very much, Mr. Jorisch.
Dr. Cook.

STATEMENT OF STEVEN A. COOK, PH.D., HASIB J. SABBAGH SENIOR FELLOW FOR MIDDLE EASTERN STUDIES, COUNCIL ON FOREIGN RELATIONS

Mr. Cook. Thank you, Madam Chairman, Ranking Members, members of the subcommittee for inviting me here to appear before you to discuss the important issue of Hamas' Benefactors: A Network of Terror.

The focus of my testimony will be the underlying political and philosophical reasons why Hamas enjoys support from Qatar and Turkey in particular. I will leave the financial issues to my two colleagues, Avi Jorisch and Jonathan Schanzer.

Let me begin with Qatar. Qatar's support for Hamas is consistent with its populist approach to the region, which is part of Doha's broader effort to establish and reinforce its policy independence from larger and more powerful actors, especially Saudi Arabia.

Qatar's $400 million investment in Gaza in 2012, at a time when Hamas was moving away from Syria and Iran over the Syrian civil war, should be viewed in a similar light to Hamas'—to Doha's $8 billion investment in Egypt from the time Hosni Mubarak fell through the ouster of Mohamed Morsi, and its support for certain groups in Libya, an effort to leverage its vast wealth to purchase influence around the Middle East.

The fact that the Qataris have tended to use their resources to support Islamist groups does not necessarily indicate that they share the violent world view of Hamas and other groups. Rumors about the former Emir, Hamad bin-Khalifa al Thani, being in support of the Muslim Brotherhood aside, it is more likely that the Qataris miscalculated the effect and extent of political changes in the region.

Like observers in the United States, Europe, Turkey, and the Arab world, Doha drew the erroneous conclusion that popular movements that brought changes in the Middle East had paved the way for new Islamist political groups in the region. That being said, believing that Islamist political movements would dominate regional politics as a result of the Arab uprisings is qualitatively different from support for Hamas, however.

Doha maintains without any irony that the sanctuary that it provides for Khaled Meshaal and others is a humanitarian issue. It also maintains that it plays an important role as a facilitator of communication between the Hamas leadership and other regional actors. This claim would be more compelling if the Qataris demonstrated they could actually influence Hamas leaders.

This isn't necessarily to excuse anything that the Qataris have done. It is not hard to notice the cynicism of Qataris who have used Khaled Meshaal's presence in Doha, their overall relationship with Hamas, as part of this broad regional competition with the Saudis, the Emiratis, and in particular now the Egyptians.

Although there is a certain propaganda value to giving Meshaal so much airtime on Al Jazeera and holding Qatar out as a defender of so-called Islamic rights in Palestine in contrast to other regional powers that implicitly support the Israeli war effort, Palestinians and Israelis suffer in the process.

Let me now turn my attention to Turkey. On a superficial level, Turkey is an unlikely supporter of Hamas. It is a NATO ally, an aspirant to EU membership. It has long had relations with Israel, and it maintains a secular political order. But there are five important reasons why Turkey is a supporter of Hamas.

First, there is broad public support among the Turkish public for the Palestinian cause. This doesn't mean that Turks support Hamas, broadly speaking. But it has allowed the ruling Justice and Development Party to ally support, legitimate support, for Palestinian rights with support for Hamas.

President Erdogan and the party from which he comes, the party's rank and file, are all anti-Zionists. Their history, their philosophy, their world view is steeped in anti-Zionism. In February 2013, in fact, then Prime Minister, now President Erdogan declared Zionism as a crime against humanity.

Third, the Justice and Development Party has long harbored what can only be described as a peculiar soft spot for Hamas. Party leaders and activists are quite open about the fact that they see themselves and their history reflected in Hamas. They built a narrative linking the Turkish Islamist movement's struggle against a repressive state and elite with Hamas and its conflict with Israel and the Palestinian Authority.

Fourth, Turkey's foreign policy activism under the Justice and Development Party has placed an emphasis on Muslim solidarity. Hamas and its conflict with Israel falls into the category of a Muslim cause, and is, thus, deserving of Turkish support.

And, finally, the strategic vision of Turkey's new Prime Minister, Ahmet Davutoglu, who previously served as Foreign Policy Advisor to the Prime Minister, and then, since 2009, as the Foreign Minister, requires support for Islamist movements around the Middle East, including Hamas.

Davutoglu, quite simply, believes that a state system based on nationalism and political institutions that trace their lineage to the West is fundamentally unsustainable in Muslim societies. If Turkey is going to lead the region, Ankara must do so as a Muslim power in cooperation with Islamist groups like Hamas.

Well, what should the United States do about this? In the context of the current regional environment, it does not lend itself to the United States taking tough actions against either Doha or Ankara. I will remind you that the President is about to announce a strategy for combating ISIS which will no doubt involve both Turkey and Qatar.

Hamas isn't going to lay down its arms against Israel, at least not in the short time horizons that policymakers have to deal with. Destroying Hamas, at least in the short term, is not even in the interest of Israel. The best answer that the United States—is to put itself in a position to actually pressure on its allies, Qatar and Turkey, to place, in turn, pressure on Hamas.

How can the United States possibly do that? First, the Obama administration has been far too solicitous toward both countries, especially Turkey. There have been denunciations from the podium in the State Department and other places of Erdogan's heated rhetoric during the recent war, but nothing from the President or the Secretary of State.

Congress has been relatively silent on both Qatar and Turkey. During the conflict this past summer, four Members of the Congressional Turkey Caucus wrote a strongly worded letter to Prime Minister Erdogan, but other than that the Congress has not had much to say on the heated rhetoric coming from Anakar in particular.

We should not allow a coming set of delegations to go to Turkey to register U.S. disapproval. There is a tremendous interest among the Obama administration to engage with the new Prime Minister of Turkey. I think that this is a mistake that is unlikely to move the Turks away from Hamas.

The suggestion that we should somehow dismantle the al Udeid Air Base is a long-term solution to a much bigger problem that Qatar presents. Unfortunately, policymakers must be realistic. The U.S. does not have the means to make support for Hamas costly in either Turkey or Qatar. We will have to accept these relations for the moment while working over the long term to go after the financing of Hamas, to build up the Palestinian Authority against Hamas, and to make the impression on our allies that support for Hamas will, over a long term, have consequences here in the United States.

Thank you very much.

[The prepared statement of Mr. Cook follows:]

COUNCIL *on*
FOREIGN
RELATIONS

September 9, 2014

Hamas' Benefactors: A Network of Terror

Prepared statement by

Steven A. Cook

Hasib J. Sabbagh Senior Fellow for Middle Eastern Studies
Council on Foreign Relations

Before the

House Committee on Foreign Affairs, Subcommittees on the Middle East and
North Africa and Terrorism, Nonproliferation, and Trade

United States House of Representatives
2nd Session, 113th Congress

Madam Chairperson and Members of the Subcommittee:

Thank you for the invitation to appear before you to discuss the important issue, "Hamas' Benefactors: A Network of Terror." The 50 day war between Israel and Hamas, which killed 2,174 people including an estimated 1,466 civilians, the vast majority of whom were Palestinians, cost billions of dollars and traumatized two populations, has focused attention once again on the Islamic Resistance Movement (know universally by the group's Arabic acronym, Hamas), its worldview, capabilities, and its patrons. It is my privilege to testify before you today about this last issue, specifically the relationship between Hamas and the governments of the Republic of Turkey and the State of Qatar.

The ties between these American allies and Hamas—a terrorist organization—contribute to instability and violence. Under political, financial, and military pressure from Israel, the United States, the Palestinian Authority, Egypt, Saudi Arabia, and the United Arab Emirates, Hamas has found relief in support from Qatar and Turkey. This has helped instill Hamas with confidence to defy the formidable group of powers that opposes the group, though there is no direct evidence that either government counseled Hamas to reject Egyptian ceasefire proposals during the recent conflict. As disturbing as the robust bilateral ties that Hamas maintains with Doha and Ankara it will be difficult for the United States to undermine these relations. There is a logic to the Qatar-Hamas and Turkey-Hamas relationship that benefits Qatari and Turkish regional interests. In the latter case, there is what can only be described as a strange affinity for Hamas within Turkey's ruling Justice and Development Party. There is a lot to dislike about Hamas' relations with the Qataris and the Turks, but we should recognize that the conduct of foreign policy is a complicated and often messy affair. Keeping that in mind, there is a potential benefit to these relationships: American officials might find it useful to leverage these ties to communicate with Hamas during times of crisis. There are, of course, problems with this approach (discussed in detail below), but these channels may be the least costly way—in terms of human lives—to stop or prevent rockets from falling on Israel and the inevitable Israeli response.

I will focus my testimony on the underlying political and philosophical reasons why Hamas enjoys support from Qatar and Turkey, the two cases I know best.

Qatar

Since the mid-1990s, the Qatari leadership has sought to use the vast natural resources at its disposal to advance Doha's influence well beyond both its modest physical size and small population. A year after Sheikh Hamad bin Khalifa Al Thani deposed his father and installed himself as Emir in a bloodless palace coup, Qatar launched al Jazeera. The network quickly captured the attention of the Arab world with its mission to tell the news through Arab eyes. The decidedly populist bent and thinly-veiled Islamist sympathies of the network's commentary combined with an unsparing view of politics and society throughout the Middle East—with the notable exception of Qatar—proved wildly popular in the region much to the dismay of Arab leaders. A staple of al Jazeera's programming, especially the talk shows that were modeled after those on American cable news networks, was criticism of the United States, its support for Israel, and its overall approach to the region. It is important to note that al Jazeera also broke a regional barrier when it included Israelis, notably government officials, in its reporting on regional issues. At the same time, Doha sought to develop closer links with Washington, constructing al Udeid air base in 1996 to host American forces that were forced to depart from Saudi Arabia. It was from this base that the United States Central Command prosecuted the wars in Afghanistan and Iraq and from where American commanders will manage any future conflict in the Persian Gulf. However contradictory these policies may seem to be, they were critical to achieving the Qatari leadership's goal of transforming the country from a sleepy backwater to an independent, regional player.

Qatar's support for Hamas is consistent with its populist approach to the region, which is part of Doha's broader effort to establish and reinforce it policy independent from its larger and more powerful neighbors, especially Saudi Arabia. This has become the *sine qua non* of Qatar's foreign policy. It is in this context that the Qataris has provided Hamas political, diplomatic, and financial support. In 2012, when Hamas began to distance itself from Damascus and Tehran over the conflict in Syria, the Qataris took advantage of this opening, offering $400 million in assistance to Gaza. This was similar in ways to the $8 billion that Qatar provided to Egypt in the period between the ouster of Hosni Mubarak in February 2011 and that of Mohammed Morsi in July 2013, and Doha's support for the Libyan Islamic Movement for Change, whose leader played a role in the military campaign against Muammar al-Qaddafi. Taken together these investments represent Qatar's effort to leverage its vast wealth to purchase influence around the Middle East. The fact that the Qataris have tended to use their resources to support Islamist groups does not necessarily indicate that the country's leaders share a worldview with these groups.

There have been rumors that the former Emir, Hamad bin Khalifa Al Thani, is a member of the Muslim Brotherhood, which would explain his sympathies for Hamas. These stories should be handled with great caution, however. They surfaced after the July 2013 coup d'état in Egypt and can be traced back to stories in the Egyptian press most of which is overtly hostile to Qatar. Without ruling out an ideological affinity between the Qataris and Hamas, it is more likely the Qataris miscalculated the effect and extent of political changes in the region. Like observers in the United States, Europe, Turkey, and in the Arab world, Doha drew the erroneous conclusion that the popular movements that wrought changes in Tunisia, Egypt, Libya, Yemen, and that threatened regimes in Syria and Bahrain had paved the way for the emergence of a new Islamist political order in the region.

Believing that Islamist political groups would dominate regional politics as a result of the Arab uprisings is qualitatively different from support for Hamas, however. Doha maintains without irony that the sanctuary it provides for Khaled Meshaal is a "humanitarian issue" and that Qatar plays an important role as a facilitator of communication between the Hamas leadership and other regional interlocutors, presumably the United States, Israel, Egypt and other Arab actors. The latter claim would be more compelling if the Qataris demonstrated that they could actually influence Hamas leaders. Despite the widely held belief in Washington, Jerusalem, and Cairo that the Qataris scuttled Egyptian cease-fire proposals, the evidence for this claim currently remains rather thin. It is based on a single, unnamed source in the London-based daily, *al Hayat*, which was subsequently picked up by *Haaretz*, the *Jerusalem Post*, *Times of Israel*, and the Egyptian newspaper, *al Ahram*.

It is likely that the relationship between Qatar and Hamas is more complicated than has been portrayed. Over its more than three decades of existence, Hamas has demonstrated that it is an independent actor, capable of calculating its own interests and pursuing its own goals regardless of its patrons' wishes. The organization's rejection of the Egyptian sponsored cease-fire likely had more to do with the quality of those proposals and the way Hamas leaders defined their political and military objectives than diktats from Qatari officials. This is not to excuse Qatar's behavior. It is hard not to notice the cynicism of Qataris who have used Khaled Meshaal's presence in Doha and the overall relationship with Hamas as part of its regional competition with the Saudis, Emiratis, and Egyptians. Although there is a certain propaganda value to giving Meshaal so much airtime on al Jazeera and holding Qatar out as a defender of Arab and Islamic rights in Palestine in contrast to other regional powers that implicitly supported the Israeli war effort, Palestinians and Israelis suffer in the process.

Turkey

Turkey seems like an unlikely patron for Hamas. It has been a NATO member since 1952, an aspirant for membership in the European Union, and maintains an officially secular political system that is designed in part to prevent the emergence of the kind of Islamist group that Hamas represents. Turkey recognized Israel in 1949, though did not upgrade to ambassadorial level until decades later. Despite the presently tense relations between Jerusalem and Ankara, the two countries enjoy well-developed economic relations. Traditionally, the Turks have positioned themselves as a neutral party in the Arab-Israeli conflict, using good relations with all the parties to advance peace.

This was a role that Ankara took up with considerable vigor after 2002 when the Justice and Development Party (AKP) came to power. The Turkish government remained largely faithful to this neutrality until early 2006. It was in February of that year when Khaled Meshaal visited Ankara. There then-Foreign Minister Abdullah Gul, other senior foreign ministry officials, and party leaders hosted the Hamas leader at the AKP's headquarters. At the time, the Turks maintained that the visit was consistent with their effort to forge peace between Israelis and Palestinians and argued that they counseled Meshaal to recognize Israel's right to exist.

After Israel's Operation Cast Lead in late 2008 and early 2009, Turkey's position has shifted from that of an interested, but neutral party to a patron of Hamas. Then-Prime Minister Erdogan was outraged over both the loss of Palestinian lives during the invasion and then-Prime Minister Ehud Olmert's failure to warn the Turkish leader of the coming hostilities during an official visit to Ankara just days before they began. This was deeply embarrassing for Erdogan who was made to look either complicit with the Israeli incursion or too weak to stop it. Yet the reasons for Turkey's shift are deeper that Erdogan's pique over a particular Israeli military operation and into five broad categories:

- There is broad public support for the Palestinian cause among the Turkish public. This does not mean that Turks are necessarily predisposed toward Hamas and its worldview, though some clearly do share its worldview. Rather, the Turks have generally demonstrated sympathy and support for Palestinian efforts to achieve statehood. This genuine and sincere support has nevertheless made it possible for the AKP to elide support for legitimate Palestinian rights with support for Hamas.

- President Erdogan, the AKP leadership, and the party's rank-and-file are anti-Zionists. The outlook of the *Milli Gorus* (National View) movement from which the AKP emerged has long harbored hostility to Israel. When the Justice and Development Party came to power it jettisoned the anti-Western shibboleths of Turkey's Islamist old guard from whom Erdogan and Abdullah Gul broke when they formed the AKP in August 2001. There was also some hope that as a reformist, modernizing party it would reject anti-Zionism and anti-Semitism as well. To Erdogan's credit, after the November 15, 2003 Istanbul bombings that targeted the Beth Israel and Neve Shalom synagogues, the Turkish government responded forcefully denouncing the bombings, reiterating the importance of Turkey's Jewish community to Turkish society, and apprehending the perpetrators. In 2005, both Erdogan and Abdullah Gul separately visited Israel. Erdogan visited the Yad Vashem Holocaust Memorial, confirmed 17 new joint military projects, and invited Ariel Sharon to visit Ankara.

  In the almost decade since his visit to Jerusalem, however, Erdogan has remained true to the political and philosophical traditions that have guided the AKP and its predecessor parties. The Turkish leader declared that Zionism is a "crime against humanity" in February 2013. The tense relationship between Turkey and Israel is not solely Erdogan's responsibility, however. Ehud Olmert miscalculated in not appealing to Erdogan for Turkey's assistance with Hamas and Gazan rocket fire prior to launching Operation Cast Lead. Moreover, the May 2010 Mavi Marmara incident was an egregious violation of international law, which left 8 Turks and a Turkish-American dead.

- The Justice and Development Party has long harbored what can only be described as a peculiar soft spot for Hamas. Party leaders and activists are quite open about the fact that they see themselves and the history of their party reflected in Hamas. They have built a narrative linking the Turkish Islamist movement's struggle against a repressive state and elite with Hamas and its conflict with Israel and the Palestinian Authority. The very fact that Hamas won a free and fair election in 2006, the results of which the United States, Israel, and the EU refused to recognize reinforces this "we-were-once-like-Hamas" account of the party's history. As a result, the AKP leadership regards itself as uniquely qualified to mentor and moderate Hamas.

  What makes the party's effort to link its own history with that of Hamas particularly strange is how at variance it is with the Justice and Development Party's rise to power and its own professed worldview. Turkish Islamists were routinely repressed from the time of the Republic of Turkey's founding through four coups d'état between 1960 and 1997 and countless other efforts on the part of state elites to ensure the security of Turkey's secular political system. Yet even with the significant pressure of the state, from the time of the founding of the modern Turkish Islamist movement in 1969, its political parties have participated in politics, joining coalition governments in the 1970s and leading a short-lived government in the mid-1990s. After each round of repression that in the Turkish context meant banning political parties and certain politicians, Islamist parties quickly returned to the political arena under new names and after a period of time their leaders were often also allowed to return. Turkish Islamists never took up arms against the state. This stands in sharp contrast to Hamas, which places a premium on violence in the effort to achieve Palestinian rights.

- Turkey's foreign policy activism under the Justice and Development Party has placed an emphasis on Muslim solidarity. As a result, Turkish diplomacy is active in traditional areas like the Balkans and the Middle East, but also Africa, where there are large Muslim populations. From the Turkish perspective, Hamas and its conflict with Israel falls into the category of "Muslim cause" and is thus deserving of Turkey's support.

- The strategic vision of Turkey's new prime minister, Ahmet Davutoglu, who previously served as foreign minister and foreign policy advisor to the prime minister requires support for Islamist movements, including Hamas. As the Turkish academic, Behlul Ozkan, make clear in an influential article in the journal *Survival*, Davutoglu's vision of a strong, powerful Turkey, leading the Muslim world is essentially an Islamist one.[1] Davutoglu believes that a state system based on nationalism and political institutions that trace their lineage to the West is fundamentally unsustainable in Muslim societies. If Turkey is going to lead the region, Ankara must do so as a Muslim power in cooperation with Islamist groups.

U.S. Policy

The Qatari and Turkish relationships with Hamas pose a policy problem for American policymakers on a number of levels. First, both Doha and Ankara are important to the United States in other arenas. As noted above, Qatar's al Udeid air base is critical to supporting U.S. military operations in the region, which given the threat of the Islamic State in Iraq and Syria may be ramping up again. Second, Turkey is also critical to managing the conflicts in Syria, Iraq, and, as a member of NATO with the second largest military in the alliance, will surely play an important role in confronting Russia over Ukraine. Finally, there is an undeniable logic, which Secretary of State John Kerry clearly recognizes, of exploiting the ties between Hamas and Qatar as well as between Hamas and Turkey as means to communicate with the organization. As noted above, in the abstract this is the least costly way of stopping or preventing further bloodshed, but there are practical problems with this approach. Neither the Qataris nor the Turks have proved that they can decisively influence Hamas.

Policymakers must also ask themselves what is it that the United States wants when it comes to Hamas? There is not an easy answer to this question. Of course, Americans would like for it to renounce violence and commit itself to peaceful coexistence with Israel, but this is altogether unlikely in the short time horizons in which policymakers exist. The best answer is that the United States wants to put itself in the best position to apply pressure on Hamas to cease rocket fire into Israel and abide by post-cease-fire "rules of the road." If that is what Washington wants then the way in which the Qataris and the Turks conduct their relations with Hamas is manifestly unhelpful, relieving pressure on the group rather than maximizing it.

As a result, broader strategic considerations should not preclude Washington from registering its disapproval with Doha and Ankara. Cooperation with Qatar and Turkey in other realms does not require quiescence when it comes to Hamas. Unfortunately, Washington does not have as much leverage with either Qatar or Turkey on this issue unless policymakers want to take the drastic step of designating both allies supporters of terrorism. It is unwise to take because it would hurt U.S. interests.

Recommendations

1. Recognizing what little recourse they have, American policymakers can still register their disapproval. The administration has been overly solicitous of both allies, in particular Turkey. The President and/or

---

[1] Behlul Ozkan, "Turkey, Davutoglu and the Idea of Pan Islamism," *Survival: Global Politics and Strategy*, 56:4, 119-140.

the Secretary of State must make clear publicly Washington's disapproval of the ties Doha and Ankara maintain with Hamas. This should not be left to spokespeople from the Department of State or the National Security Council. Although these dedicated professionals communicate the U.S. government's positions and policies, I am afraid that public censure will only register with the leaderships of the countries if they are done at the highest levels. There is not much else that can be done regarding Qatar, which is in a position of relative strength given the importance of al Udeid to the United States military.

2. Congress has been silent on both countries' relations with Hamas. The United States may have little leverage with the Qataris, but that does not mean that Congress should refrain from makings its views known. During the fighting in Gaza, the co-chairs of the Congressional Caucus on U.S.-Turkish Relations and Turkish Americans conveyed a sharply worded letter to then-Prime Minister Erdogan for "remarks...widely viewed as anti-Semitic and are most definitely anti-Israel," but there has been no Congressional statement or any other action related to Turkey's robust relationship Hamas. Absent the Obama administration willingness to hold Ankara accountable on this issue, there is clearly an opportunity and need for the Congress to do so.

3. Specifically regarding Turkey, there is interest across U.S. government agencies, notably the State Department, Defense Department, and Commerce Department, in engaging with the new Davutoglu government in Turkey. One notable example is the planned late September visit to Turkey by the President's Export Council. The Secretary of Commerce is slated to lead that delegation with other senior officials from her department. This visit and other visits should be canceled to register Washington's disapproval of Turkey's relationship with Hamas. Although the AKP (and virtually every other political party in Turkey) traffics in anti-Americanism, these visits are valuable to the Turkish leadership, which regards them as a sign of U.S. approval of the policies of both the government and the party. The Obama administration regards these trips as an opportunity to engage Turkey's new prime minister. Yet Davutoglu's vision is in part the intellectual framework for Turkey's overall problematic approach to the Middle East, which includes good ties with Hamas.

Policymakers should be realistic. Registering American disapproval over the relationship between Qatar and Hamas and Turkey and Hamas is unlikely to alter policies in Doha or Ankara. These ties serve both Qatari and Turkish regional interests. Unfortunately, Washington does not have the ability—primarily because the United States needs Qatar and Turkey on other policy issues—to make these relations costly for Doha and Ankara. More than likely the United States will have to accept this reality and try to use the ability of these government to communicate with Hamas in an effort to establish a stable, less violent relationship between Israel and the Gaza Strip.

Ms. Ros-Lehtinen. Thank you very much.

I will start with the questions and answers. Dr. Cook, I find your testimony troubling. You said, ''We will have to accept these relationships.'' And in your testimony you state that the U.S. has little to no leverage over Qatar or Turkey, pointed to repeatedly the al Udeid Air Base in Qatar as giving Qatar the position of relative strength in U.S.-Qatari relationship, yet Dr. Schanzer and Dr. Jorisch point to this as a point of leverage in favor of the U.S.

You state, ''There is not much else that can be done regarding Qatar, which is in a position of relative strength given the importance of Udeid to the United States military.'' The United States may have little leverage with the Qataris about Turkey. Your recommendation is that the Secretary of Commerce should cancel a visit.

And you state, ''Unfortunately, Washington does not have the ability, primarily because of the United States needing Qatar and Turkey on other policy issues, to make these relations costly for Doha and Ankara. More than likely, the United States will have to accept this reality.'' That is pretty depressing, and I think that we do have a lot of leverage.

Giving Qatar support for terrorist groups—Hamas, ISIL, the Muslim Brotherhood, and others—it is very—in its very contentious relationship with some of the Gulf nations, I would ask the gentlemen if there is a way of leveraging what we have, plus our relations with the Gulf nations to press Qatar to abandon its support for terror. If so, why, and why has the administration taken the position of appeasing Qatar instead of condemning it for supporting terrorism.

And the latest events in Gaza have rehashed the problem of appeasing Qatar instead of the Unity Palestinian Authority government. And thank you for pointing out how we have got to make sure that that divorce happens. What is Hamas' role, and what will it be? Hamas has no intention of recognizing Israel or making peace with the Jewish state. It is a U.S.-designated state sponsor of terrorism.

There are laws on the books—I was the author of one—that would preclude any U.S. funds from going to any Palestinian Government that included Hamas. Thank you for your recommendations about cutting off funding.

And, Dr. Schanzer, you have done extensive research into the Fatah-Hamas relationship. And as you answer your questions from members, because I won't have enough time, i hope that you will further explain those financial ties between the Palestinian Authority and Hamas, and whether it is possible that U.S. money has indeed been going directly to Hamas, or indirectly.

We know that Hamas used to get a lot of its money from taxing goods that entered Gaza from the smuggling tunnels, and they taxed residents also of Gaza, and of course from its patrons like Turkey and Qatar. We also know that it receives funds from other sources, like front companies and charities, and Mr. Meadows had asked about that.

The Treasury has done a pretty good job of countering Hamas' fund-raising activities, but more can still be done. If you could at times that our members will ask questions, somehow walk us through the network of charities and front companies and how this money finds its way into the hands of Hamas.

But let me just, in my remaining 1 minute, have your take on whether we do have leverage or not over Qatar and Turkey.

Mr. SCHANZER. Madam Chairman, thank you. I would say that we do have leverage. I think that, number one, to conduct an assessment of what it would take to leave al Udeid and to create a new base, whether in—I have heard options such as the UAE or Erbil or perhaps other places where we know that allies would be interested in doing this.

I think even alerting the Qataris that we are interested in having these assessments done, either by the GAO or by the Pentagon, I think would send the exact right message to the Qataris that they will not enjoy the protection of the United States forever, so long as this relationship continues with Hamas.

The other thing that I would note here is that we know that there are entities within the Qatari Government or within—that are based in Qatar, Qatari nationals, that are involved in supporting Hamas. We have to date not designated them. This could send shockwaves through the Qatari financial system. It would be a signal to banks around the world, to countries around the world, that Qatar has been tainted in the support of this terrorist organization. We have done this in the past with other terror groups and other countries——

Ms. ROS-LEHTINEN. I am sorry. I am out of time.

Mr. SCHANZER. Sure.

Ms. ROS-LEHTINEN. And I would just point out, one last note, that the Qatari Foundation, or whatever they call themselves these days, was one of the sponsors of the Congressional baseball game. Shame on us. With their name in lights, yikes. So we should start pointing fingers at ourselves.

Mr. Deutch is recognized. Thank you.

Mr. DEUTCH. Thank you, Madam Chairman. I am just going to pick up where you stopped, Dr. Schanzer. You have—the panel has spoken about the budget. We have often focused on charities, but the specific focus on Qatar and their contribution to somewhere between a $500 million and $1 billion annual budget, how does the money flow? Where does it go? What banking institutions does it go through? And compare that to the way that we treat the banking system when it accepts the money of other terrorist groups, so that we might get some guidance on how to proceed from a policy standpoint, Dr. Schanzer.

Mr. SCHANZER. Sure. Ranking Member Deutch, this is a difficult question to answer, and I think that is primarily because it is not like Hamas is settling up at the end of the year with Ernst & Young and declaring how they move their money. I mean, this is— obviously, this is a clandestine terrorist organization.

We have some hints about how some of this money is moved. For example, there was the recent attempt to transfer $60 million from Qatar to the Arab Bank in Jordan. They of course declined that transaction. This was just a couple of months ago once the Unity government had been forged, and that was turned down.

We also have been aware of a practice known as bulk cash smuggling through the tunnels connecting the Sinai Peninsula to the

Gaza Strip. This is a very fancy way that Treasury describes basically carrying suitcases or trash bags full of cash under those tunnels to replenish the banks in the Gaza Strip.

There is all sorts of money laundering, over invoicing, under invoicing, sort of classic money laundering techniques, as well as perhaps even some straightforward transfers with bank accounts that appear to be legitimate with connecting countries. So there is lots of different ways that Hamas moves this money, but a lot of it is dealt in cash and that—but I should just note that this is the result of Treasury's successes.

We have driven Hamas' finances underground, and to a certain extent we are now victims of our own success because it has made it harder to track.

Mr. DEUTCH. Right. But, Mr. Jorisch, $500 million or $1 billion, that is a lot of plastic bags and suitcases. I mean, how do we track it?

Mr. JORISCH. Ultimately, I agree with Dr. Schanzer. Much of the cash is going through the tunnels or was going through the tunnels, but ultimately the way the banking sector works is setting up correspondent bank accounts.

Ranking Member Deutch, I don't know where you bank, but let us assume your account is at Citibank. Just like you have an account at Citibank, Citibank has correspondent accounts all over the globe. It is called the correspondent account. Qatar has correspondent accounts all over the globe, including having Qatari financial institutions that have correspondent accounts here in the United States.

If we really wanted to send shockwaves through the Qataris and Turkey, simply say to them, ''Your financial institutions have to go through an added level of due diligence when going through the U.S. financial sector.'' One, FINCEN, part of the Treasury Department, could issue a financial advisory that simply states, ''Qatar and Turkey are helping Hamas and other terrorist organizations launder their money,'' also sending shockwaves through the financial sector.

And, finally, leveraging international organizations such as the U.N. and the Financial Action Task Force, which is the international body for money laundering in terms of finance, and have our U.S. delegation push them to add them to specific lists, basically ensuring that their access to the international financial sector is hampered.

Mr. DEUTCH. I appreciate that. I just have 1 minute left, Dr. Schanzer.

So, Dr. Cook, let me just ask you, you talked about regional competition. You talked about Qatar trying to announce its policy independence from Saudi Arabia. Can you—just in the remaining time I have, can you speak to the relationship between Qatar and the other nations that it is trying to separate itself from? And why is that happening? And, ultimately, how does that rift play into our hands of trying to stop the flow of funds to terrorist groups?

Mr. COOK. Thank you very much for the question, Ranking Member Deutch. Qatar is engaged in a competition with the larger, arguably more powerful countries in the region. In particular, it has a pathological problem with the Kingdom of Saudi Arabia. There has been an effort over a long period of time, but over the last w decades in particular, in order for the countries to establish their independence. Al Jazeera and its kind of unfettered look at the rest the region is part of reinforcing that independence.

Funding groups that are not approved by the Saudis, the Emiratis, on the other hand of an issue, is a way in which the countries have sought to pursue a populist foreign policy and a way in which it has sought to reinforce this independence. That is, in part, the reason why the countries have invested as much as they have in, for example, Hamas, although all of the money that—this $500 million to $1 billion budget does not all come from the Qataris, not to excuse their behavior.

But as Dr. Schanzer pointed out, the Treasury has been successful in literally driving Hamas underground. A good portion of that budget comes from smuggling under tunnels on the Sinai frontier in which Hamas collects taxes. There is an argument to be made that if you didn't have those tunnels, and you opened up those borders, Hamas would suffer financially because they wouldn't be able to tax at the kind of rate that they have.

But, nevertheless, it is a policy conundrum for the United States and others how to go—exactly go out there. Do we try to shut down the tunnels? It increases funding for Hamas. How do we deal with Qatar, a country that in the short run, as we are about to undertake additional military operations in Iraq, as we are about to leave Afghanistan, as we are about to potentially expand military operations that include Syria, a place from which we are going to prosecute hostilities in the region.

I will remind you and the members of the subcommittees that it was in 1996 that the United States abandoned its bases in Saudi Arabia, because the Saudis kicked U.S. forces out of the Kingdom. And it was in Qatar that the countries built this facility for the United States.

So over the short run, in the next months or years, abandoning operations at al Udeid are not feasible, and that is why this leverage that we are talking about is not as great as it seems in the abstract.

Thank you.

Ms. Ros-Lehtinen. Thank you very much.

Pleased to yield to our subcommittee chair, Mr. Poe, Judge Poe.

Mr. Poe. Thank you, gentlemen. I appreciate especially the fact that all of you not only have answers, you have plans, excellent ideas on a plan. Excellent. I thank you for that. We ought to take them all and implement as many as we can.

There is a couple of things that I see. One, direct money going to Hamas, and then indirect money from the United States going to Hamas, and I would like to talk about the second one first.

The United States gives money to the Palestinian Authority. Is that correct? The Palestinian Authority uses money to pay terrorists who are in jail in Israel, and the more serious the crime that this terrorist, Hamas terrorist, has committed against Israel or Israeli citizens, the more money they get. Is that true? You can say yes or no or explain. We will go down the row.

Mr. Schanzer. It is a bit more complicated, Chairman Poe. In light of the most recent Unity government that was created, as I understand it, the PA knew that this was going to be a problem, and it was—and in order to head off that problem they moved the office that deals with this to the PLO and got it out of the hands of the PA.

The PLO is of course not within the jurisdiction of the United States. We don't fund it. We don't have much influence over it. And, in fact, their funding is a black box. We don't—you know, we still don't know where it comes from. And so it is my understanding that they have moved the financing of these people who are now sitting in Israeli jails to the PLO.

Mr. POE. So, but the Palestinians—Palestinian Authority does not pay it, the Palestinian—who pays that money to Hamas terrorists who are in jail? I know they get paid to go to prison because they have committed a terrorist act. That is kind of——

Mr. SCHANZER. So we believe right now that it is the PLO, although I think it is still not clear. It is not exactly as if the Unity government has had time to take form and for the bureaucracies to have shifted. The intent was back in I guess it was April or May when the Unity government was formed, the intent was to move it over to the PLO. It would be an interesting question right now to query the PA to find out whether they have in fact moved that or if it still sits within the PA.

Mr. POE. All right. Mr. Jorisch.

Mr. JORISCH. And I would counter by saying money is fungible, sir. And when money goes from the United States to the PA, ultimately you are swapping out one dollar for another. We are by happenstance—not even by happenstance, but we are funding these activities from taking place.

Mr. POE. And I am speaking specifically about paying Hamas terrorists to be in prison. And the more serious the crime, the more money they get. Is that correct? Are they paid by the Palestinian Authority or the Palestinians for these terrorists when they are in jail in Israel?

Mr. JORISCH. They are paid by—as Dr. Schanzer pointed out, originally they were paid by Hamas. And the Unity government came into place, these funds may have moved to an outside entity. But ultimately when they commit terrorist attacks, yes, their families are paid a significant sum of money on a monthly amount. Yes, sir.

Mr. POE. Do you find that a bit alarming?

Mr. JORISCH. I find it more than alarming. I find it disturbing and reprehensible.

Mr. POE. And the more serious the crime, the more people maybe they kill, the bigger—more amount of money they get for themselves or their family. Is that correct as well or not?

Mr. JORISCH. The larger the crime, the more they get?

Mr. POE. Yes.

Mr. JORISCH. I can't say that I know, sir.

Mr. POE. Anybody else can answer that? Dr. Cook, do you know?

Mr. COOK. I am going to do something very un-Washington-like and say I do not know, sir.

Mr. POE. Thank you very much. Qatar and Turkey, what approximately is the percentage of money that Hamas receives from these two countries? So their operating expense is—they have 100 percent. How much of that 100 percent is from Qatar or from Turkey? And Turkey, excuse me.

Mr. SCHANZER. Well, if you add up the annual $400 million that we believe has been pledged by the Qataris, and perhaps the rumored $300 million provided by the Turks, then you are looking at $700 million out of what was roughly a $1 billion budget. And this actually goes to—I want to just briefly——

Mr. POE. Is that 70 percent?

Mr. SCHANZER. That would be 70 percent. Yes, sir.

Mr. POE. Okay.

Mr. SCHANZER. I am no math major, but I would actually just note, and this was—I wanted to add this on to my response to Mr. Deutch, that we believe that because of what has happened in Egypt that budget has dropped precipitously. That it could be now that Hamas is operating on a $300 million or even $350 million budget, I mean, we are really—we are talking about now 35 percent, using that math again, of that original budget.

That is significant, and in many ways that could have been the reason why they launched this war, to basically fight for the ability to have those tunnels either reopened or to have the border opened. That may have been their strategy. In fact, according to some former colleagues of mine, that is exactly what they decided to do after that Arab Bank transfer was declined.

Mr. POE. How many tunnels are there or were there?

Mr. SCHANZER. Well, there have been 1,700 that have been shut down on the EU border.

Mr. POE. Okay.

Mr. SCHANZER. Thank you very much. I yield back.

Ms. ROS-LEHTINEN. Thank you very much.

Mr. Sherman of California.

Mr. SHERMAN. Did you say 1,700?

Mr. SCHANZER. I did.

Mr. SHERMAN. Glad our record is clear. One other thing to clarify for the record, and that is that just because we have a military base in Qatar does not mean we have to defend that regime or that country. And last I heard, we have a base in Guantanamo. I know some members of this committee who do not believe that we should defend the Cuban regime from whatever external or internal threats it faces. You know, it wouldn't be a bad thing to get rid of the al Thani family and keep the base.

We have got a proposed $11 billion military sale, looking at the weapons that Qatar is acquiring in that transaction, but their overall military posture. Are they posturing themselves to defend themselves from an attack from Iran, from Saudi Arabia, or to project power outside their own borders?

Mr. SCHANZER. I should just say up front—I will be very un-Washington, too—I am not a military expert. But I can tell you that we have an analyst working on this to compile the list. And point number three of my testimony on page 16, it is the full list of the military deals that are pending, the $11 billion.

Some of this material will be used certainly for defense, the ability to shuttle forces quickly to the spot of an attack, anti-missile batteries, things of the like, but also Apache attack helicopters, which have dual use.

I would not propose right now to say that the Qataris are looking to go on the offensive in the region. I think they are trying to upgrade their military to——

Mr. SHERMAN. Thank you. Do the other witnesses have a comment on that? I would point out that the UAE appears to be involved in bombing Libya, and so small countries can project power. In light of Qatar's support from Hamas, should we be approving and proceeding with this $11 billion sale? Dr. Cook? Maybe I could get a yes/no from all three of you.

Mr. COOK. I don't think we should be proceeding with the sale. No.

Mr. SHERMAN. Mr. Jorisch?

Mr. JORISCH. No, sir. I don't think we should be proceeding with the sale.

Mr. SHERMAN. Mr. Schanzer?

Mr. SCHANZER. Nor do I.

Mr. SHERMAN. One of the difficult things is there seems—there is general support for providing aid to the people of Gaza, and those people are held hostage by, and any dollars—Hamas—any dollar that goes into Gaza could be grabbed by Hamas.

Now, I would point out that by U.N. statistics, the health and life expectancy of the residents of Gaza is better than that of the residents of Turkey, but—so we may be providing more aid, and we are providing more aid as a world than any other needy population in the world. But everyone agrees that at least some aid should read the people of Gaza.

Israel collects a value added tax and tariffs on goods going into the West Bank and Gaza, gives that money to the PA. Does Hamas—who gets that money or the portion of it relevant to value added taxes and tariffs collected by Israel on goods legally going into Gaza?

Mr. SCHANZER. Ranking Member Sherman, that is—about $100 million per month that goes directly to the PA Government in the West Bank. The way that they——

Mr. SHERMAN. And that is on goods both headed to the West Bank and goods headed into Gaza.

Mr. SCHANZER. Well, we have got a significant drawdown in terms of what is going into the Gaza Strip. But, yes, I think there is a small portion of that; obviously, a larger portion going to the West Bank.

Mr. SHERMAN. Right.

Mr. SCHANZER. I couldn't tell you on the exact percentages, but at the end of the day there is money that is trickling through—the payment of officials on the other side, the Palestinian Authority officials, that continue to be paid there. Some of them may be aligned with Hamas, but, more importantly, there is the—and I have actually flagged this for this subcommittee before. The electric company that is operating out of Gaza has been funded almost entirely by the West Bank government, and Hamas collects the bills for that, and they do not remit it back. So this is an indirect way——

Mr. SHERMAN. So money is collected by Israel, it goes to the PA, and in various ways that benefits Hamas. Dr. Cook, do you have a comment on that?

Mr. COOK. My sense is—and, again, I—the expertise in the flows of—financial flows is with Mr. Jorisch and Dr. Schanzer. But my understanding is, of course, that the Israelis collect this value added tax and then contribute it to the Palestinian Authority. That Palestinian Authority uses it as it sees fit. So it——

Mr. SHERMAN. Including methods that help—because I want to get in one final comment, and that is one of our possible responses to Qatar is to call for democracy in Qatar, in which the ruler of the country would be selected not only by those who are ''citizens'' but anyone who has lived there legally for 10 or 20 years.

We are talking about a country with over 2 million people, 80 percent of whom are guest workers. And I don't know of any supporter of democracy that would say you could exclude 80 percent of the population of a country from voting and call it a democracy. And we have had some difficulty with promoting democracy in the Middle East, but if there is one place where I don't think it would result in a worse government it would be Qatar.

I yield back.

Ms. ROS-LEHTINEN. Thank you very much, Mr. Sherman.

Pleased to yield to Mr. Perry.

Mr. PERRY. Thank you, Madam Chair.

And thank you, gentlemen. The testimony is fascinating. It is my understanding that United Sates taxpayers give approximately $300 million to the United Nations Relief and Works Agency annually in order to provide humanitarian assistance. And during the recent conflict, rockets were discovered in three of UNRWA schools. I can remember the wailing and the moaning about Israel bombing these schools, and I also remember the U.N.'s spokesperson deriding those actions.

In one of those cases, UNRWA handed over to local authorities the rockets in the Hamas-run territory, and in another the rockets disappeared. Can I just get your comments on the relationship between you and UNRWA and Hamas, and what we can do to ensure that this—it is unbelievable to me. It is unimaginable that we, as taxpayers, then watch the criticism from the U.N. in particular. In particular. I can understand Hamas; it feathers their own nest. I mean, it furthers their goal and they do it specifically for that reason. I understand that. The U.N., $300 million in taxpayer money.

Let us start with Mr. Cook and just go down the line.

Mr. COOK. Thank you for the question, sir. UNRWA, as it is often referred to, is a deeply compromised organization, and it has been for some time deeply compromised by its relationship with various different groups and been caring for Palestinian refugees now for 60-plus years, and over that time has become compromised by its association with different groups.

In the Gaza Strip in particular, UNRWA workers are either compromised by their—let us say their dispositions toward Hamas or are intimidated by them. And, as a result, that is how you get these bizarre situations in which UNRWA staff are handing rockets over. They are either compromised by supporting them——

Mr. PERRY. Please provide briefly your solution set at the same time.

Mr. COOK. Well——

Mr. PERRY. What should the United States do, in your opinion?

Mr. COOK. Well, I think that the solution is, obviously, to either not fund UNRWA or to build up the Palestinian Authority, so that it can take care of people in the Gaza Strip, something that we have thus far been unwilling to do, but, nevertheless, it is a solution to the problem.

Mr. JORISCH. In short, defund UNRWA. UNRWA is engaging in horrific activities. It is aiding and abetting a terrorist organization. It is essentially allowing Hamas to store its rockets. The Israelis are left holding the bag. They don't really know what to do with themselves. Essentially, they have to choose between protecting their own citizens and ultimately hurting civilians on the other side.

There is a cycle of violence here that, really, there is very little that one can do. Defund UNRWA, simply put.

Mr. SCHANZER. Representative Perry, I would actually just back up for a moment and note that in my view UNRWA has played a very peculiar role in perpetuating the Palestinian-Israeli conflict. It has changed the definition of ''refugee'' such that you now have the—you have the children, the grandchildren, and the great-grandchildren of the original refugees.

So whereas there were roughly 800,000 refugees after 1948, today, by their calculations, there are 5 million refugees. There is no way, obviously, that Israel could accommodate them. In reality, there is probably something like 30,000, which is obviously a number that Israel could deal with, but UNRWA has not yielded on that. That is one area of reform that I think is absolutely necessary.

But in terms of its direct support to Hamas, look, they are beholden to the people who control that territory. They are beholden to that government. They have to operate under Hamas rules. This means that in some cases the schools teach Hamas curriculum. Sometimes they hire Hamas as employees, and we have seen examples of this.

The fact that they were allowing for the building of tunnels, these commando tunnels, underneath their facilities in my opinion very much needs to be investigated, if not by these committees by some other, to determine whether there is culpability.

There is—actually, most people don't know this, but there appears to be what I would only call a lobby office here in Washington. Why a refugee agency needs to maintain that here in Washington is still beyond comprehension to me.

And so, look, in answer to your question, we either need to have a serious overhaul of this organization, or to defund it and let it collapse. It has got to be one or the other, and this has been a problem that has gone on for too long.

Mr. PERRY. Thank you. It would be fascinating, as my time expires, to know what this administration in the form of our Ambassador to the U.N. has done in this regard. I have heard nothing from the counterpoint side, and a strong statement or more from this administration to say it is unacceptable to the U.N., which we are great part of and the United States funds in a great degree, and yet we have no—we are saying nothing. We are silent.

And I yield back. Thanks, Chair.

Ms. ROS-LEHTINEN. Thank you very much.

Mr. Connolly.

Mr. CONNOLLY. Thank you, Madam Chairman.

Mr. Jorisch, I find myself certainly in agreement with much of your analysis, but I am concerned about your prescription. If I heard you correctly, your answer is defund UNRWA, defund the Palestinian Authority, put more pressure on Qatar, make their banking system harder, close the military base in Qatar.

I am a little concerned that if we did all of that we—and maybe we should—but we certainly actually lose leverage, and it seems to me that we also leave the region, imperfect instruments though they may be, and even at times counterproductive instruments, with very little left with which to try to address a very complex and painful and difficult situation. Those seem pretty rigid, absolute prescriptions.

Mr. JORISCH. Sir, ultimately, we have to know who our friends are and who our friends are not, send the right messaging to who our friends are not. We have a tremendous amount of leverage over Qatar. We have a tremendous amount of leverage over Turkey and others in the region, and we don't leverage it. When it comes to our banking sector, they need us more than we need them.

And I have a feeling, and I know for a fact having spent time in government, when you exert that pressure those governments move.

Mr. CONNOLLY. That is sometimes true. But I guess I don't share the view that you are either a friend or you are not a friend. I think the world is more complicated than that. In fact, I would argue that is part of the underpinnings of the Bush administration foreign policy that did not work.

Dr. Cook, Mr. Jorisch just made reference to our leverage, a lot of—considerable leverage in Turkey. What leverage would that be, in your view? And, by the way, I appreciate your calling out the letter that the four co-chairs of the Turkey Caucus here in Congress wrote to Prime Minister, now President Erdogan. I was proud to be one of those four. And I think, frankly, President Erdogan has gone far afield, and I think we have got a problem now, given the fact that he has a new job.

And of course ironically he used the letter publicly to help himself, which is always what I am concerned about, that when we make some strident statement here, it actually has a counterproductive effect—not that that is our intent—politically there. And we saw that certainly with Erdogan.

But help us understand. What is the leverage? I mean, if I follow Mr. Jorisch's prescriptions, let us close the bases in Turkey, let us kick them out of NATO, not that he said that, but that is where leads us, that logic. You are either a friend or you are not. You either do what we want or you don't. And if you don't, we are going to look at the absolute punishments available to us. Is that really the leverage we have over Turkey?

Mr. COOK. Thank you for the question, Mr. Connolly. And I think that what your remarks reflect is the difficulties, the way in which we talk about leverage. We make assumptions that we have leverage in certain areas when we don't necessarily have them. As you point out, that very strongly worded letter on which you were a cosigner, Erdogan turned around and used very much to his advantage.

Mr. CONNOLLY. And by the way—I am sorry to interrupt—but for the record, we did not release the letter. It was a private letter to the Turkish Government and to him. He released the letter.

Mr. COOK. Exactly, exactly.

Mr. CONNOLLY. Because we were trying to show respect to—one last-ditch effort to get him to cease and desist and recall that virulently anti-Semitic language. And of course he decided to just use it for his own political gain.

Mr. COOK. And that is precisely the case. And it is not just Erdogan and the ruling Justice and Development Party that he uses this type of anti-Americanism to advance their political agenda across the Turkish political spectrum.

Mr. CONNOLLY. But do we have leverage? I mean, how much of a threat is it really that we will close down the bases, we will——

Mr. COOK. Right. I think it is unlikely to have an effect on Erdogan, the threat that we would leave Incirlik Air Base, from which we are using for a variety of purposes with regard to Iraq and Syria and only going to grow in more importance as we get reengaged on those conflicts.

I think what I pointed out in my testimony, something that Erdogan does in fact respond to, and that he does respond to public censure from senior U.S. Government officials. With all due respect to our State Department spokespeople, they are dismissed when they make statements criticizing Erdogan for the type of anti-Semitic language that he used.

And I should point out he even used language that is deeply offensive to Americans asking rhetorically what Americans knew about Hitler. The answer is 200,000 Americans died fighting Hitler.

But when the President of the United States—on the occasion that he has used the public censure of Erdogan, when the Secretary of State rebuked Erdogan directly for his statement Zionism is a crime against humanity, we saw some change in their behavior.

These kinds of threats—I think the Turks know we are not going to leave Incirlik Air Base. I think the Turks know that we need them to—by dint of their geography on a number of regional hotspots. That is not to excuse their behavior.

As I said in my testimony, there is a bizarre, a peculiar connection between the Justice and Development Party and Hamas, and it has got to stop. That said, I think those kinds of threats—Mr. Jorisch and Dr. Schanzer have a better view of the financial issues that are important in these types of relationships. That may in fact be something where the United States has leverage, but these other kinds of threats strike me as—and with respect to my colleague and friend, strike me as things that are not necessarily going to move President Erdogan or his new Prime Minister.

Mr. CONNOLLY. Thank you. Thank you, Madam Chairman. And I apologize to the panel, I wish we could have more—I only have 5 minutes—because I know this conversation really has much more depth to it, and many more aspects to it. So thank you all for——

Ms. ROS-LEHTINEN. Thank you very much.

Mr. Clawson is recognized.

Mr. CLAWSON. I have a more short-term question for the three of you, please. In this recent 50-day conflict, Hamas has shot lots of rockets, right? And it is my belief that the Israeli Defense Organization have also destroyed some of their rocket-making manufacturing. So now, is Hamas resupplying? I mean, we have been talking about money. You know, more money means more rockets to Hamas, which means more rockets into Israel.

So are they resupplying? Where are those rockets coming from? And what can the U.S. do to stop it? Or if we can't stop it, how can we work with Israel to slow it down? I would like to hear what you have to say.

Thank you.

Mr. SCHANZER. Mr. Clawson, thank you for the question. It was our understanding before the conflict began that there were roughly 10,000 rockets in Hamas' possession. It fired off roughly 4,000 of those rockets into Israeli airspace. Another estimated 2,500 were destroyed through Israeli operations targeting the rocket caches below ground or perhaps even some of them before they were being fired, even as they were on the launcher.

And so that leaves us with about 3,500 rockets in their possession, a lot of them smaller rockets, the smaller ordnance. Maybe about 200 of those mid-range rockets, the M302s or Fajr 5s, still remain in Hamas' possession.

The resupplying of the smaller range rockets, the Qassam rockets, the Grad rockets, and even possibly the ones that they call the J80s, and perhaps even a few other varieties, are being rebuilt again thanks to Iranian engineers who have trained Hamas on Iranian soil to be able to put these together.

So, in other words, they smuggle in these small bits of whatever they need for the rockets. Sometimes they use materials that are already there, including plumbing, piping, and other things that can be, you know, dual use. And so they have this indigenous rocket-making capability right now. It is the longer range rockets that I think the Israelis are more concerned about in terms of what was—what could be smuggled in, and it is for that reason that they are keeping a very close eye on the fishermen.

You know, if you remember, the terms of the cease fire deal included the ability for the fishermen to go further out at sea. The concern is is that some of these fishermen are fishing for other things, bringing back rockets into the Gaza Strip. Of course, the tunnels remain a problem. Even though a lot of them have been destroyed between Sinai and Gaza, some of them are still operational, and that is—so at least some of those rockets are still getting in.

And, of course, as I mentioned before, Sudan remains a significant pipeline. Port Sudan I believe is the area that we all need to focus on right now. That is the hub for where Iranian rockets arrive before they are smuggled up into Egypt and across the Sinai Peninsula.

Mr. JORISCH. Mr. Clawson, I totally agree with Dr. Schanzer's analysis. But ultimately, while we have been leveraged, we do have—and this is to Mr. Connolly's question as well—lies strictly in the banking sector. When it comes to correspondent banking, ultimately each and every one of these financial institutions—Iranians, Sudanese, Qatari—all want a presence in the United States, all rely on the U.S. dollar. And our largest presence lies in whether we allow those financial institutions to have a presence in the United States and/or their third party transactions.

So take a Sudanese bank or an Iranian bank. They are using European financial institutions, which essentially will allow them access to the U.S. dollar. Ultimately, our largest leverage lies with the financial sector. There is no financial institution in the world that doesn't want a U.S. presence and/or access to the U.S. dollar.

When we talk about moving the dial, the Turks and the Qataris, in particular, they want access to the United States. During Dr. Schanzer's time and mine in the Treasury Department, we had repeated meetings with the Turks in terms of their status in the United States and with the FATF, the Financial Action Task Force. And I can assure you they moved very quickly when the FATF or the United States thought about, spoke about, even made intimations that it was going to be on a blacklist. And that does move the dial.

Same thing when it comes to the Sudanese and the Iranians. The Iranians, the found it much, much more difficult in large part as a result of Congress, the CISADA, the Comprehensive Iran Sanctions Accountability and Divestment Act, to essentially move money around the international financial sector.

Financial institutions around the globe stopped doing business with them. In 2010, before CISADA was passed on July 1, 2010, there were 59 banks around the globe doing business with Iran's financial institutions. Afterwards, that number came down to maybe a dozen, maybe half a dozen, somewhere between half a dozen and a dozen financial institutions.

There are those out there, policy analysts on both sides of the Atlantic, that essentially say that in large measure the reason why the Iranians are at the negotiation table today are in large part because of those sanctions.

Mr. CLAWSON. If I can jump in just for a second. Moving money around in a multi-national organization, of which I have experience, is not easy to do. There is tax laws and regulations from the different—from all of the different originating countries.

It feels like other than with the exception of Iran we are not really trying that hard. Is that right? Because——

Ms. ROS-LEHTINEN. Mr. Clawson, that is an excellent question, and maybe the panelists will have an opportunity to——

Mr. CLAWSON. Thanks, guys. Great job.

Ms. ROS-LEHTINEN. Thank you. Thank you, sir.

Mr. Schneider of Illinois is recognized.

Mr. SCHNEIDER. Thank you, Madam Chairman. And, again, thank you for calling the hearing, and the panel for helping us dig deeper into a very difficult situation.

Dr. Cook, you seem to draw a distinction or try to draw a distinction between—specifically Qatar, between ideology and a desire for influence. The ideology of Hamas stems directly from its outgrowth from the Muslim Brotherhood. How important, in your view—I will open it up to the whole panel—is the Muslim Brotherhood ideology to the funding of Hamas from Qatar, from Turkey, from even individuals and others in the region?

Mr. COOK. Thank you. It is a very, very important question, and I think the events in Egypt during the summer of 2013 have generally colored the way in which we view the Muslim Brotherhood and its popularity throughout the region.

It had been quite popular in Egypt, and then suddenly wasn't, and I think that there is an assumption that people make that the Brotherhood is on its last legs, on its heels throughout the region, when in fact I think private citizens, people throughout the region, do subscribe to a world view of the Muslim Brotherhood, and that is a function—and the funding that comes from not just Qatar but comes from all over the Middle East to Hamas and other organizations around the region are a function of the fact that the Brotherhood and its world view remain important in the politics of the region.

There is no doubt that there are Brotherhood networks throughout the region. One of the demands that the Saudis and the Emiratis have of the Qataris is that they return Saudi and Emirati members of the Muslim Brotherhood that have found sanctuary in Doha.

It is something that is I think deeply embedded and ingrained throughout the region. It is widely seen as legitimate. And Hamas, as a result, is widely seen as legitimate. Remember, this organization is referred to as Resistance. And in many ways many of the people who are—especially those private groups and private donations coming in, see Hamas' legitimate resistance against the Israeli occupation.

Mr. SCHNEIDER. So, and, Mr. Jorisch, I see you nodding your head. Is there a relevant distinction between the Muslim Brotherhood driven ideology of Hamas and al-Qaeda or Islamic State? Aren't they all part of the same line of ideology?

Mr. JORISCH. The answer is absolutely yes, sir. If you look at the ideology of Hamas, and you look at the ideology of Islamic jihad, and you look at the ideology of al-Qaeda and ISIS, they are one and the same, and they have an ideology of essentially implementing the Islamic State not only in their own jurisdictions but growing it.

There is Dar al-Islaam and Dar al-Harb. There is the Abode of Islam and the Abode of War. And each of these organizations is playing off of the exact same playbook, and which is why I find it so bizarre, so strange that the administration is effectively calling for war against ISIS on the one hand but negotiating or encouraging the negotiation with Hamas on the other. It makes no sense. We ought to have a policy on radical Islam, and we don't have one today.

Mr. SCHNEIDER. Dr. Schanzer?

Mr. SCHANZER. Yes. Mr. Schneider, it is a very good question. Look, I think the way that Qatar is traditionally described in this town is pragmatic. I think it ignores the fact that—Qatar is in fact also a Wahhabi organization or a Wahhabi State. It is not in the same vein as Saudi Arabia, but it is certainly imbued with a certain Islamist ideology.

And so we have seen not only the support of Qatar for Hamas or for the Muslim Brotherhood, but also for the Musra Front, other jihadi groups, in Syria the Taliban as we know. And, look, I would just point out also that—and this does not get a lot of attention, but Khaled Sheik Mohammed, the mastermind of the 9/11 attacks, lived in Qatar with the full knowledge of the Qatari Government for several years. And before the United States was about to take him out on Qatari soil in an operation, he was tipped off and he was able to leave.

This is the kind of country that we are dealing with. And, yes, it is pragmatic in the sense that it is willing to buy large stakes in real estate ventures here in the United States, or other companies around the world, the fact that it has money to burn in the Western economy does not make it an equal partner ideologically.

Mr. SCHNEIDER. Right. And I am sorry to take back the time, but I only have a few seconds. But it is that natural resource wealth leading to an ideology that has a broad reach across the entire region.

And in the last seconds, and maybe we can submit answers later, or if there is time available, you have got the Muslim Brotherhood ideology coming in direct conflict with facing Iran. But Iran—this is not a case I believe of our enemy of our enemy is our friend. These are both issues that we need to address and stand up to. And while they fight each other, we need to know and understand our relationship vis-à-vis each as well.

And I see I am out of time.

Mr. WEBER [presiding]. The gentleman yields back, and the gentleman from Florida, Mr. DeSantis, is recognized for 5 minutes.

Mr. DESANTIS. Thank you, Mr. Chairman.

Thank you for the witnesses. I have really appreciated hearing your testimony and your answers to the questions. And I think following up on that last series of questions, and I think, Mr. Jorisch, you really hit it on the head to point out to the extent to which Hamas is part and parcel of the other Islamic jihadist movements that we are seeing.

Hamas wants an Islamic caliphate, correct?

Mr. JORISCH. Absolutely. Yes.

Mr. DESANTIS. I mean, the idea that somehow they just—they are fighting against occupation is what people will somehow say. Of course, we know Israel left Hamas almost a decade ago, or left the Gaza Strip. They had a chance to govern themselves. They chose to elect Hamas.

What did Hamas do? Did they try to turn it into a Singapore on the Mediterranean? No. They built terrorist tunnels. They purchased rockets. The infrastructure that was left behind by the Israelis, they raised and destroyed rather than use that.

And so they have had opportunities, and to me when those people say, "Oh, it is just the Israeli policy that they are responding to" fundamentally misunderstands the ideology that motivates them. Do you agree?

Mr. JORISCH. I don't understand how we can be silent when it comes to Hamas when we are so loud when it comes to al-Qaeda and ISIS. It makes no sense. We should learn from 60 years ago to listen to what our enemies are saying. Hamas broadcasts clearly its ideology in its newspapers, on its radio stations, and its television statements. Hezbollah does exactly the same.

As Mr. Schneider pointed out, in this case it is not under the enemy of our enemy is our friend. Hamas, the Sunni jihadi organizations, and the clerical regime that rules Iran today effectively are paying, when it comes to the issues that we care about, off of the same playbook. The same playbook.

Mr. JORISCH. Absolutely. And that is why I appreciated the comments about the UNRWA funding. I have a bill, the Palestinian Accountability Act, that dealt with all of these issues. Any relationship in the government with Hamas, funding would stop.

UNRWA, unless it could be demonstrated that they are on the up and up, funding ceases. And I think that that—it is a sense of, okay, some people say the world is complicated, but do you want to reward bad behavior, or do you want to punish bad behavior?

And so for me it is simple. If I see UNRWA hiding rockets in one school, ''Oh, we didn't know,'' then another, ''Oh, we didn't''—so, I mean, at some point, you know, it is just—it doesn't even pass the laugh test. And so I think it would, one, be a good judicious use of protecting the taxpayer by not sending that funding over there; and, two, it would also just be a statement of our values. You align with Hamas; you are clearly not interested in peace with Israel. You are certainly not interested in being a constructive force in the region, so then we should act accordingly.

I think the Secretary of State should have cut off the funding. I think the chairwoman's amendment she passed several years ago mandated that. They had kind of said, ''Oh, well, Hamas doesn't have undue influence.'' But as you point out, money is fungible. The money that goes to PA they can say is not going to be sent to Hamas, but it frees up other funds that can go there.

With Turkey, to what extent is it tenable to consider them to be an ally. Of course, they are in NATO. The idea was they are a bridge from kind of the West to the Middle East. They had played a constructive role and have been pro-Western in the past. Under this current President, they have gone in a very, very bad direction.

So how should we respond to Turkey? I know some of you said pressure Turkey. But can you have somebody in NATO who is also funding Islamic jihad? I mean, wouldn't that just completely rule you out of being an ally of the Western democracies?

Mr. COOK. I assume that is a question for me. Thank you for it. I think that you raise some very serious questions about the Turkish Government under the Justice and Development Party and new President Erdogan, who was the Prime Minister over the course of the last 12 years.

The Turks maintain that they want to have a 360-degree foreign policy, which means their connections, they are robust connections to the West, as well as connections to other countries in the region. My concern is, however, that they themselves are not being true to that 360-degree foreign policy, and that under the new Prime Minister Ahmet Davutoglu, who is the architect of their foreign policy over the course of the last decade, believes Turkey to be a Muslim power. And, as a result of its—the role he believes it should play, requires that Turkey support groups like Hamas and others in the region.

I think that it is up to NATO to determine whether Turkey has run afoul of what constitutes being a NATO partner. Certainly, what's going to happen in the coming weeks, days, and months with regard to the Islamic State of Iraq and Syria, and the conflict in Iraq, that will be a test of whether Turkey takes its NATO role very seriously.

Thus far, they have said that they are playing a non-active role in this coalition. I am not exactly sure what a non-active role in a coalition exactly means, but I think that the question that you asked, Mr. DeSantis, about Turkey and its ultimate trajectory is a very good one.

Mr. DeSantis. Thanks. I am out of time, but I appreciate everything that you guys have given us to consider today, and I yield back.

Mr. Weber. Thank you.

The gentlelady from Florida is recognized.

Ms. Frankel. Thank you, Mr. Chair. And I think we all agree that despite the fact—and we are grateful of the cease fire—that Hamas remains a threat.

Since I am sort of at the end of the questioning here, and this has been a great discussion, I would sort of—I would like to ask you if you can just sort of sum up what we have heard in little bits and pieces. And if you could, as best possible, looking at the four named countries that you say are the—or maybe the benefactors, our four—yes, Qatar, Turkey, Iran, Sudan—if you could describe simply what you think are the motivating factors of why they are benefactors. Is it anti-Semitism, religious, economic, whatever, and what are our best leverage points in cutting off the funding?

Mr. Schanzer. I can maybe take a first stab at this, Ms. Frankel. Thank you. Look, I think that, first of all, the anti-Israel sentiment, the Islamist sentiment, these are kind of the lowest common denominators in all four of these countries.

Each of them come about it from very different perspectives. Iran, I think a much more vitriolic brand; Sudan, I think somewhat subservient to Iran in that respect; Qatar and Turkey, more of the Muslim Brotherhood variety of this ideology. But, nevertheless, this resonates not only within the populations but also across the Muslim world. So this is an attempt to demonstrate leadership across the region as well as at home. And this I think continues to drive this activity.

Now, as for how to handle this, we I think have really leveraged quite a bit of sanctions already on Iran, quite a bit on Sudan, and there are—look, I think there may be some juice left in the tank with the Iranians. I think there are still ways to pressure them. The Sudanese, probably less so; they are a basket case.

But with regard to Turkey and Qatar, I don't think we have even started to try. I don't believe that we have sent the tough messages. I don't believe that we have designated the one-off individual or one-off bank that can send that shockwave through the system.

There is a way to turn this up one notch at a time to let these countries know that once you have done one designation, if they don't fix things, then you do another, and then you do another.

This is, by the way, what we did with the Iranians which led them to the negotiating table over their nuclear program, and eventually it got so painful that they decided that it was time to talk.

We have not—I mean, we continue to hear that we have no leverage. I think this is very wrong. I don't think that we have even started to try to see whether we have leverage. I think the time is now to start.

Mr. JORISCH. I yield my time to Dr. Cook. I agree completely with Dr. Schanzer's sentiment.

Mr. COOK. Thank you for the question, Ms. Frankel. The basis for Qatari and Turkish support are—for Hamas are laid out in some detail in my written testimony. But it is a combination of both pragmatism, regional politics, and domestic politics that—essentially to support advances, particularly Qatari and Turkish interests.

I think that as long as that logic holds, it is going to be difficult for the United States to undermine those relations. I certainly believe that in the short run our leverage, given the roles that both the Qataris and the Turks are playing in the region, and are going to play in the region, our leverage is more limited than my two colleagues would suggest.

Over a long period of time, if the United States wants to consider moving its air bases from Qatar or moving a NATO facility, both the Incirlik Air Base, as well as the early radar warning missile system that is directed against Iranian ballistic missiles out of Turkey, those are the kinds of things that the United States and the Congress can explore in terms of gaining some leverage, as well as the kind of financial actions that Dr. Schanzer is discussing.

But, unfortunately, I think for the short term, for the time horizon that this administration is looking at, and for the challenges that it faces in the region, the kinds of things that have been suggested in terms of leverage are not likely to come about.

Thank you very much.

Ms. FRANKEL. Thank you, Mr. Chair, and I yield the rest of my time.

Mr. WEBER. Excellent questions. Although I am a little miffed because you took one of mine.

Okay. The Chair now recognizes Dr. Yoho.

Mr. YOHO. Thank you, Mr. Chair.

Thank you, gentlemen. I appreciate the testimony. It has been enlightening, and I feel your frustration because what you are recommending is what we should have been doing and we haven't done. And for the last 30 or 40 years, when we look at what we have done with Mubarak and Egypt, knowing these tunnels are being built and we are giving money, and this veneer of democracy that they are building and are promoting, are allowing the terrorist acts to go on.

And when you look at, like, Turkey's new Prime Minister, Ahmet—I can't pronounce his last name—believes that the state system, based on nationalism and political institutions that trace their lineage to the West, is fundamentally unsustainable in Muslim societies. If Turkey is going to lead the region, Ankara must do so as the Muslim power in cooperation with Islamist groups.

I mean, it pretty much lays it right out there. The new Prime Minister says this. And so knowing that, and if we have been playing this game for—I don't want to call it a game. If we have been—our foreign policy, which I think is way off track, it is askew, it is a broken compass, because we don't have strong national leadership directing this for what America stands for.

If we don't stand up and say, "This is what we want to do," the Palestinian Authority—in fact, we have got a resolution on what we were talking about earlier. Paying $500 million a year over the last 10 years is $5 billion of the American taxpayers' money, and they have—and this is from 2010—their resolution in the Palestinian Authority, Government Resolution 21 and 23, where they are paying the prisoners in Israeli prisons for acts of terror. It goes up to $3,400 a month. Average income over there is $4,000 a year, and we are promoting this.

We know we are promoting it, and it is—the money is fungible. It is like Mr. DeSantis says, if we give $500 million here, even though it doesn't go there, it frees up money coming from somewhere else. And I think it is time to draw a line and just say, "We are not putting up with this anymore," and put the pressure on Qatar and Turkey and just say, "We are not going to help you work against us." If we are serious about bringing peace to the Middle East, I think your recommendations are spot on, and we will promote introducing those as far as legislation.

Other than that, Dr. Cook, you basically stated that—what I got out of your last statement, that Turkey—they want that 360-degree vision, you know, all-encompassing. It is kind of like they want their cake or our cake and eat it, too. You know, they are taking it with one hand—and we see this so often. They take money—these countries take money from us with one hand, and then cover up their eyes with the other and ignore the problem. And the American taxpayers are the one on the hook, and our military are on the hook.

And if we are to bring world peace, we need to act like the superpower that we are and just say, "We are not doing this anymore." And if Turkey and Qatar don't come to our side, I say we need to just put more pressure on them and go after the money, because I think the money is the thing that is the most important.

And I just want to say I appreciate you guys being here, because I think you—like I said before, you are spot on with your testimony. We look forward to act on that.

Thank you. I yield back.

Mr. WEBER. The Chair recognizes the gentleman from Georgia, Mr. Collins.

Mr. COLLINS. Thank you, Mr. Chairman. It is always hard to follow someone who has such a lack of passion for his issues as Dr. Yoho does, a dear friend of mine who has actually—I think it was really interesting—and before I get into the questions here, Dr. DeSantis, you hit on this, and I think personally—I know there is going to be a big speech tomorrow night. I am glad we are speaking and the world is shivering—tomorrow night about what we are wanting to do.

But I would love to see a lead on sort of what you said earlier is the financial aspect of what we can do. I mean, as someone who has served at al Udeid, who has been at that base, who has been in Iraq, who has been, you know, back and forth here, I have got some other questions. But your comment hit me, and if anybody could—if anybody wants to—why don't we—is there more of a concerted effort we could lead with cutting the funds off.

If we could lead in these areas, whether it be Qatar, Saudi Arabia—I mean, let us talk about—let us just lay it on the table—these areas where we could do the funding sources through "charitable organizations, non-charitable"—that seems to me, you are right. Iran came to the table. There has been a lot of discussion in this room about, oh, now we have pivoted and we are—we let them off the hook.

We are letting them do exactly what they want to do. We gave them some money, and they are spending that money in ways that we can't be accountable to. So that—I want to just real quickly touch on that as far as a first piece strategy in our dealings with ISIS right now.

Mr. SCHANZER. Thank you, Mr. Collins. First of all, with respect to Iran, I do believe that the sanctions that we have imposed certainly brought them to the table. There is no question about it. I think it became very painful for them over time. This was, again, that strategy of turning it up one notch after another. I think the swift sanctions in particular, or pushing them out of the swift system, I think was probably the final step that forced Iran to come to the table.

I do believe now that the sanctions relief that we are offering Iran, more than $7 billion, has certainly helped them spark a resurgence in their economy, and that is certainly taking away some of our leverage. And, by the way, I should just note in the context of Hamas, as we give them these billions of dollars, and as they are shipping these weapons over to Hamas, we are indirectly subsidizing this. We are allowing for it to happen, and I think it is a big mistake.

Mr. COLLINS. Well, I think that has been brought up, and "indirectly" is too kind of a word. You might as well just say, "We are directly doing it, and we are fighting on two fronts here." That is another hearing that we could have. You know, we have been through it, and I appreciate your answer, but I want to turn to Hamas and I want to turn to a specific incident that—and all of you can comment on this.

And this goes back to The New York Times reporting, an article about the three Israeli teenagers that were kidnapped in occupied West Bank in June. We know they were victims of a Hamas operation, supposedly without the foreknowledge of Hamas leadership. But according to Israeli investigators, two men associated with Hamas carried out the kidnapping and subsequent killing after receiving $60,000.

Now, they were—this was—the money was flown from—you know, basically flew—or flowed from Gaza Strip to the West Bank in five installments, you know, the five installments clearly not raising red flags. There is an issue here that we could look at.

The question I have is—and for any of you to sort of look at here—is Israel—with Israel allowing such restricted travel outside of Gaza, let us talk for a moment how that money would have flowed, because I think that goes to the heart of some of this funding, not only for Hamas but ISIS. I agree with you completely; let us call everybody what they are, and let us just don't put one in another—can you speak to that? Any of you want to touch on that one?

Mr. JORISCH. There are four primary means that you can basically move money. You have cash, you have the formal financial sector, you have the informal financial sector, and you have trade. I don't know which of those means were used, but let us just take them each at a time.

The cash is very simple. You basically put it in your pocket, you swallow it, you have it in a suitcase, what have you. You have the banking sector, so theoretically you could have had some coming out of an ATM, you could have had a wire transfer, you could have had a check, et cetera.

Mr. COLLINS. And let me stop you, because given the travel restriction, don't you believe that probably the banking sector or some other kind of sector probably was more at risk or more active here?

Mr. JORISCH. I actually suspect it was probably trade.

Mr. COLLINS. Trade.

Mr. JORISCH. Or cash.

Mr. COLLINS. Okay.

Mr. JORISCH. So let us take this bottle here, and I am going to tell you that it is worth $1.

Mr. COLLINS. Right.

Mr. JORISCH. Okay? And if I ship 12,000 of these, you have got $12,000 that moves, essentially sell it on the other side. There is a tremendous amount of reporting these days that Hamas is reliant more and more on trade because we have squeezed them on the banking sector. These tunnels have now been destroyed, or the vast majority of them, so the amount of cash that can go through, more and more they are depending on over, under, and false invoicing.

Mr. COLLINS. Okay. Well, I appreciate it. And, amazingly, time has got out here. This is something that could be discussed and needs to be discussed more openly, because we are—you know, we can't isolate ourselves from the world. That is a fact.

But also, we have got to be very smart on how we strategically put assets, both material assets and human assets, in these areas in which basically we are playing both sides off the middle. And that is not—and I appreciate, Dr. Cook, all of you here today, for doing that.

And, Mr. Chairman, at zero, I yield back.

Mr. WEBER. Let the record show you were actually 1 second over.

Mr. COLLINS. Mr. Chairman, it was because of my north Georgia accent that just was so fast getting in there it just missed the——

Mr. WEBER. The gentleman yields back, and the gentleman from South Carolina is recognized.

Mr. WILSON. Mr. Chairman, thank you very much, and thank all of you for being here and providing some level of clarification. It is so sad to me this administration I think began with obfuscation, that it would say we are in a global war on terrorists. And then we get into, well, it is overseas contingency operation.

By the time the American people figure out what is going on, we will have further attacks. And so I want to thank you for clarifying. What we are dealing with are terrorists, these people who have a keen interest in killing every Muslim that disagrees with them. So it is not just Jews, not just Christians, not just Hindus. It is so universal; it is just horrifying, although it is encouraging.

I have been to the Middle East to see the Persian Gulf States, other examples. I have had—two of my sons served in Iraq, and the extraordinary people there who do want to live in the 21st century. I had another son serve with Bright Star in Egypt, and my youngest just got back from Afghanistan. And so there is hope, but we have got to show resolve.

And, gosh, it is so frustrating to me, we get into semantics. The discussion this week as I came back, is it ISIS or is it ISIL? No, it is terrorists. And so thank you all for trying to clarify this to the American people.

As we look at this—and, Mr. Jorisch, you already referenced it, but it is trade-based money laundering. And so the money to Hamas, through overpricing, undervaluing, whatever, there was an example of plastic buckets that cost $970 each from the Czech Republic. Really, we know they are really good buckets, but not like that. And so there was money that is being passed. How can we preemptively break this system?

Mr. JORISCH. Mr. Wilson, thank you for your sons' service to begin with, and I will take your first point and then move to the second. President Bush declared this a war on terror. With all due respect to President Bush, you can't fight a tactic. We learned in World War II that you fight ideologies or countries. In World War II we fought Nazism, Communism, Fascism. We fought Nazi Germany. We fought Japan. We didn't fight German U-Boats, and we didn't fight Japanese Kamikaze airplanes.

This administration, for its part, has refused to recognize that we are fighting radical Islam. And until we have a coherent, comprehensive strategy, as we did in the Cold War, when it came to a chess-like game, we are playing checkers and radical Muslims are playing chess. And until we have established a coherent policy on radical Islam, we are going to be behind the eight ball, and your sons, unfortunately, will be going to places without a coherent strategy.

To your second point, trade-based money laundering, the only comprehensive strategy that we have established is something called the Trade Transparency Unit, which essentially collects information, trade information, imports and exports, and compares them to the other side of the invoice.

Now, the United States Government has helped establish a number of these trade transparency units in places like Mexico, Colombia, Brazil, and a number of other places. We might consider funding a number of other trade transparency units in places like Israel and in Europe, which we have not done to date.

Mr. WILSON. And, again, I just thank you for raising that. And my visits—I have been to the Middle East now 12 times, and it is always encouraging, the people that we meet with. They really do want to be in the 21st century, and you identify it correctly—radical Islam, a small percentage. And so I am just very hopeful.

And last year I appreciate Dr. Fred Kagan was right here in June, and presented a map showing the spread of the terrorist organizations across North Africa, Middle East, and Central Asia. And it was extraordinary, because at the same time the administration was saying that terrorism was on a retreat. At the same exact time, indeed, Dr. Kagan was correct.

But even that, we get into semantics. I still distribute that map, and people say, "Well, actually, it is out of date because it doesn't mention ISIS or ISIL." Well, it doesn't need to, because of the changing names every day. It is international terrorism that we have got to face.

And I want to thank all three of you for, in a very positive way, raising this. But I am just so hopeful for the people of the Middle East, that working together with them we can address which is a threat to the American people.

Thank you.

Mr. WEBER. Thank you.

The Chair now recognizes himself. I have got a three-part question, really, and Lois actually asked, I think, one part of it. If you were going to—and I am going to go to each of you individually, and we are going to do it in sections. If you could—if you are going to call out countries that: A) supported Hamas; B) supported jihad, which someone argued is one and the same; and, three, are working toward a caliphate, okay, if you were going to identify countries that met those three criteria, what countries would you identify?

Let us start with you, Dr. Schanzer.

Mr. SCHANZER. Well, I think the four countries that we have identified here today all do it on some level, and I think the important thing is to note that they are doing it in varying degrees and perhaps——

Mr. WEBER. And that is my second part of the three-part question. Rank those in order.

Mr. SCHANZER. Well, look, I think Iran poses probably the most serious threat and is supportive of the most number of terrorist organizations around the world. I think Qatar has played a dangerous role similarly. Sudan has been more of a bit player, primarily because of its lack of resources. And Turkey is just new to the game.

Mr. WEBER. Okay. Do you all agree with that? Dr. Cook?

Mr. COOK. Sure.

Mr. WEBER. Okay. How do we effectively call them out and make them pay a price to change that strategy?

Mr. SCHANZER. Look, with Iran and Sudan, we have already done that, right? We have called them state sponsors of terrorism. We have got sanctions, regimes, against them, and we have taken measures to isolate them. And I think we have done a fairly effective job, maybe not effective enough with regard to Iran and its nuclear program, but certainly we have given it a good college try.

With regard to Qatar and Turkey, we have not even started to call them out. I can't stress this enough. We know that Hamas operatives are operating there in the light of day, and we know that money is flowing from these two countries to Hamas. We know, by the way, that there is other support that they are providing to other terrorist organizations in Syria right now, the same groups that we are trying to combat, and in some cases their policies have led to the rise of ISIS.

That border policy on Turkey—I mean, again, it has been one of the most dangerous things I have seen in the last 2 years, and the Turks have gotten away with it. They continue to—I think to have a loose border policy.

These are all issues that I think we have neglected to say publicly. The moment we begin to do that is I think the moment that these countries begin to second-guess the policies that they have adopted. I think that up until now it has been the quiet approach, asking them nicely. That has not worked. It is time to step up the pressures.

Mr. WEBER. Mr. Jorisch?

Mr. JORISCH. I agree. When it comes to Iran, Mr. Weber, Iran is the most dangerous player out there. They fund not only Hamas, they fund Hezbollah, tens of millions of dollars go every year—rather, hundreds of millions of dollars a year go to Hamas, hundreds of millions of dollars go to Hezbollah. If you rank them by order, you have Iran, as Dr. Schanzer points out, which is number one, and the rest in falling order of importance.

We are not leveraging our banking sector enough. We have not——

Mr. WEBER. So you would say that that is the top chair, whether we would want to bring a U.N. resolution, whether we would want to do other things, make the statement from the administration and/or Congress. Don't want it to be said that Congress wasn't doing anything. Well, that is a shock.

You would say that—do it through the banking system, number one.

Mr. JORISCH. Yes.

Mr. WEBER. Number two?

Mr. JORISCH. Ironically enough, we don't actually have an effective messaging system to that part of the world. Our television station that broadcasts into the Arab world today, not terribly effective. The radio station that broadcasts into the Arab world today, not terribly effective either. Until we basically flood the Arab media—and I mean Al Jazeera, el Arabia, and others, with some of the smartest guys in the room, to articulate U.S. foreign policy, we are not playing the game.

Mr. WEBER. Okay. Dr. Cook?

Mr. COOK. Let me say that I am in general agreement with what Dr. Schanzer has said on these issues, but I want to broaden it. And I think we should understand that not only is it just Qatar or Turkey or Iran, but it is individuals throughout the region that are contributing to these groups, to Hamas, to ISIS, to all kinds of jihadi groups. And that makes it a bigger problem than just censuring one or the other or ranking these countries.

Mr. WEBER. So do you designate those individuals?

Mr. COOK. I think that in certain places we do have to designate certain individuals who do it, but I think that the idea that we can get after every single one of them is a fool's errand. It is important——

Mr. WEBER. Well, obviously, you can't get after them, to use your term, but, I mean, you can take them—they can't visit certain countries. You can do all of those things.

Mr. COOK. I think the large numbers—with respect, sir, with the large numbers of people who do contribute to these groups, I think it is beyond the scope of everybody that we could designate.

My point in raising it is to suggest that this is a larger problem than just either one government or another government or not. Let me also amplify something that Dr. Schanzer said. I think that we have been, as I said in my written testimony, far too solicitous of the Turkish Government.

He and I disagree—he and I disagree over whether the Qataris are pragmatic or not, but the Turks have in a sense taken this on in an ideological kind of way, in their support for Hamas. And the administration has put too much emphasis on private communication. As Dr. Schanzer said, their border policy has been terrible. The kind of rhetoric coming out of Ankara from the most senior leaders of the government have created an environment of hostility in the region that has done nothing but advance their own domestic political agenda.

I think it is important for the United States to call them out on that issue in particular. I don't think, though, that we should fool ourselves into believing that once we do that that they are going to change. I think it is important for us in terms of our values and what we stand for in order to do those things, but it is not necessarily going to make them change.

Mr. WEBER. Okay. Well, I am out of time, so we are going to conclude this hearing. Thank you for your testimony. We appreciate you all.

[Whereupon, at 12:11 p.m., the subcommittees were adjourned.]

APPENDIX

MATERIAL SUBMITTED FOR THE RECORD

JOINT SUBCOMMITTEE HEARING NOTICE
COMMITTEE ON FOREIGN AFFAIRS
U.S. HOUSE OF REPRESENTATIVES
WASHINGTON, DC 20515-6128

Subcommittee on the Middle East and North Africa
Ileana Ros-Lehtinen (R-FL), Chairman

Subcommittee on Terrorism, Nonproliferation, and Trade
Ted Poe (R-TX), Chairman

September 2, 2014

TO: MEMBERS OF THE COMMITTEE ON FOREIGN AFFAIRS

You are respectfully requested to attend an OPEN hearing of the Committee on Foreign Affairs, to be held jointly by the Subcommittee on the Middle East and North Africa and the Subcommittee on Terrorism, Nonproliferation, and Trade in Room 2172 of the Rayburn House Office Building (and available live on the Committee website at www.foreignaffairs.house.gov):

DATE: Tuesday, September 9, 2014

TIME: 10:00 a.m.

SUBJECT: Hamas' Benefactors: A Network of Terror

WITNESSES: Jonathan Schanzer, Ph.D.
                 Vice President for Research
                 Foundation for Defense of Democracies

                 Mr. Avi Jorisch
                 Founder
                 Red Cell Intelligence Group
                 (*Former Policy Advisor, Office of Terrorism and Financial Intelligence, U.S. Department of the Treasury*)

                 Steven A. Cook, Ph.D.
                 Hasib J. Sabbagh Senior Fellow for Middle Eastern Studies
                 Council on Foreign Relations

By Direction of the Chairman

The Committee on Foreign Affairs seeks to make its facilities accessible to persons with disabilities. If you are in need of special accommodations, please call 202/225-5021 at least four business days in advance of the event, whenever practicable. Questions with regard to special accommodations in general (including availability of Committee materials in alternative formats and assistive listening devices) may be directed to the Committee.

COMMITTEE ON FOREIGN AFFAIRS
MINUTES OF SUBCOMMITTEE MARKUP

MINUTES OF SUBCOMMITTEE ON _____ *the Middle East and North Africa* _____ MARKUP

Day___ *Friday* ___Date_____ *7/25/14* ___Room_____ *2172* _____

Starting Time ___ *9:46 a.m.* ___ Ending Time ___ *10:15 a.m.*

Recesses | *0* | (___to___)(___to___)(___to___)(___to___)(___to___)(___to___)

Presiding Member(s)
Chairman Ros-Lehtinen

Check all of the following that apply:

Open Session ☑   Electronically Recorded (taped) ☑
Executive (closed) Session ☐   Stenographic Record ☑
Televised ☑

BILLS FOR MARKUP: *(Include bill number(s) and title(s) of legislation.)*
H.RES. 665, CONDEMNING THE MURDER OF ISRAELI AND PALESTINIAN CHILDREN IN ISRAEL AND THE ONGOING AND ESCALATING VIOLENCE IN THAT COUNTRY;
H.CON.RES. 107, DENOUNCING THE USE OF CIVILIANS AS HUMAN SHIELDS BY HAMAS AND OTHER TERRORIST ORGANIZATIONS IN VIOLATION OF INTERNATIONAL HUMANITARIAN LAW.

COMMITTEE MEMBERS PRESENT:
Chairman Ros-Lehtinen, Ranking Member Deutch, Reps. Chabot, Cotton, Schneider, Frankel, Connolly, and Grayson.

NON-COMMITTEE MEMBERS PRESENT:
None

STATEMENTS FOR THE RECORD: *(List any statements submitted for the record.)*
None

ACTIONS TAKEN DURING THE MARKUP: *(Attach copies of legislation and amendments.)*
The en bloc items were agreed to by voice vote, and the measures, as amended, were ordered favorably reported to the full Committee by unanimous consent.

RECORDED VOTES TAKEN (FOR MARKUP): *(Attach final vote tally sheet listing each member.)*

Subject	Yeas	Nays	Present	Not Voting

TIME SCHEDULED TO RECONVENE _____
or
TIME ADJOURNED *10:17 a.m.* _____

_____
Subcommittee Staff Director

Statement for the Record
Submitted by Mr. Connolly of Virginia

Throughout its history, Hamas has demonstrated that it is an organization that serves the narrow purpose of violence above all else. From its promises of government administration to its dealings with Israel and the Palestinian Authority, Hamas has sacrificed even basic human needs to its violent mission. Since its origins as an opposition force to Yasser Arafat's secular Fatah movement, Hamas has cultivated its own brand of violent insurgency to galvanize broader support for its anti-Israeli activities. With Hamas, violence is both a means and an end.

The U.S. has identified Hamas as the perpetrator of attacks on Israeli civilian and military targets by means of suicide bombings, improvised explosive devices, shootings, and rocket launches. It is with this in mind that on October 8, 1997, the U.S. Secretary of State designated Hamas as a foreign terrorist organization in accordance with section 219 of the Immigration and Nationality Act. This designation is applied with the stated intention that it will, among other things, "stigmatize and isolate the organization internationally, and deter donations or contributions to and economic transactions with the organization."

At today's hearing, we will examine how Hamas has sustained its mission despite consistent and ongoing efforts to marginalize and disarm the organization.

As I mentioned previously, Hamas has on repeated occasion used armed conflict to build support for its violent brand of opposition. When even Palestinian rivals have opted for engagement, it has drawn a line of distinction with its competitors through armed attacks. It did this as the Palestinian Liberation Organization (PLO) negotiated with Israel under Yasser Arafat, and it has occupied a similar niche opposite President Mahmoud Abbas. This dynamic changed little even under the auspices of the unity government formed in June 2014, and it was on full display during the recent conflict with Israel.

It is estimated that Hamas currently operates with an annual budget of $500 million - $1 billion. The official 2014 budget submitted by the Hamas government in Gaza totaled $894 million. As has been the case in previous years, domestic revenue was projected to cover roughly 30% of expenses. Before the unity government was formed, Hamas government employees went without a paycheck for four months. However, as Operation Protective Edge began, Hamas mustered the resources for a sustained conflict and fired thousands of rockets indiscriminately at Israeli civilian targets even as the conflict exacted a significant cost on the people and infrastructure of Gaza.

Traditional terrorism funding sources, some of which Hamas has pioneered, partially make up the organization's budget deficit and fund the capabilities that perpetuate conflict. Tax assessments on local populations, international fundraising, self-generated capital via criminal activity, and support from foreign states have all been identified by the U.S. Department of the Treasury as ways in which Hamas funds its activities. Iran, the traditional heavyweight in the field of terrorism financing, is actually challenged for supremacy in the effort to fund and arm Hamas. As Under Secretary for Terrorism and Financial Intelligence David Cohen stated in March, "distressingly, Iran is not the only state that provides financial support for terrorist organizations. Most notably, Qatar, a longtime U.S. ally, has for many years openly financed Hamas."

The U.S. has been careful to cultivate a diversity of alliances around the globe predicated on a variety of interests and needs. Alliances that require the U.S. to balance our security interests and those of our allies with immediate strategic needs cannot go untended. In the case of Qatar, we acknowledge support for Hamas while relying heavily on the operation of al Udeid Air Base west of Doha. We must continue to project that a strong relationship with the United States is in and of itself a path to influence and economic prosperity. Where that is in doubt, our terms must be clearly explained. A supportive relationship with a foreign terrorist organization is simply not appropriate for allies of the U.S.

Hamas is a particularly troubling cause. The role it plays in the Israeli-Palestinian conflict creates a multiplier effect for its propensity to stoke anger and bolster the recruitment efforts of terrorist organizations in the region. I look forward to hearing from our witnesses today on how our bilateral and multilateral relationships can be strengthened to the detriment of organizations like Hamas. There is little purpose served in providing standing or credibility to organizations that exist to perpetuate conflict.